Praise for *Tactical Communication, Third Edition*

"As an academy instructor, the most important skill I can teach cadets in a new career of law enforcement is communication. The training based on *Tactical Communication* should be mandatory in all law enforcement academies. The skills learned in the program are invaluable when it comes to learning the socioeconomic differences of the communities that we serve, and they help us better understand and communicate with the citizens we come into contact with on a daily basis."

–Sergeant Daniel G. Gutierrez, Lucas County
Sheriff's Office – Corrections Center, Toledo, Ohio

"We are committed to building trust and positive relationships with all segments of the community. The trainings based on *Bridges Out of Poverty* and *Tactical Communication* are necessary steps in reframing the relationship that the residents of Saginaw have with the police and in developing the community-oriented policing that our community deserves. It gives the officers a realistic approach to communicating with all of our citizens."

–Chief Robert Ruth, Saginaw Police Department, Saginaw, Michigan

"I consider myself a well-rounded officer with very solid safety tactics and above-average communication skills, which is why I was skeptical about what *Tactical Communication* could add to my tool belt. I walked in intending to pick apart the concepts and ended up embracing them. The training is so in-depth that it helped me realize some of my own 'hows and whys.' *Tactical Communication* is a must-have for every first responder."

–Officer Charles V. Sims, Perrysburg Police Division, Perrysburg, Ohio

D160066?

THIRD EDITION

TACTICAL COMMUNICATION

Effective Interaction Tools for First Responders

Pfarr, Jodi R., with contributions from Angel A. D.
  Tucker and Gary D. Rudick
  *Tactical Communication: Effective Interaction Tools for First
  Responders.* Third Edition.
  174 pp.
  References pp. 155–160
  ISBN: 978-1-948244-45-9

  aha! Process, Inc. ■ P.O. Box 727 ■ Highlands, TX 77562-0727
  (800) 424-9484 ■ (281) 426-5300 ■ Fax: (281) 426-5600
  Website: www.ahaprocess.com

Book design by Paula Nicolella
Cover design by Perich Design LLC

Printed in the United States of America

Grateful acknowledgment is made to J Pfarr Consulting for permission to reproduce the images on pp. 112, 115, and 116. Images and their explanations copyright J Pfarr Consulting.

Grateful acknowledgment is made for permission to reprint copyrighted material, including numerous charts and graphs, from *A Framework for Understanding Poverty* by Ruby K. Payne, *Bridges Out of Poverty* by Ruby K. Payne, Philip E. DeVol, and Terie Dreussi-Smith, and *Getting Ahead in a Just-Gettin'-By World* by Philip E. DeVol.

THIRD EDITION

TACTICAL
COMMUNICATION

Effective Interaction Tools for First Responders

Jodi R. Pfarr

**With contributions from
Angel A. D. Tucker
and Gary D. Rudick**

Table of Contents

Introduction

This book is written for first responders. First-response personnel have a difficult job as they are continuously called upon to work within many communities of different economic status. When people's economic status influences their access to our societal system, it affects the experience people have in society. That experience shapes how many things, including emergency services, are viewed and treated. First responders who have worked in all three economic communities (poverty, middle, and wealthy classes) can testify to being viewed and treated differently within each of these communities. The deeper the understanding first responders have of these differences, the safer they can keep themselves and the communities they serve.

Emergency service is particularly challenging because first responders are constantly called upon to work outside of the economic classes they are used to. When first responders, like anyone else, see things operate in a way that does not reflect their own experience, it is hard for them to make sense of the situation.

When people see things that do not make sense and are not immediately understandable, our human nature is to react to it. Any first responder will tell you that is a dangerous place to be.

This book is not meant to justify or judge the behaviors one might witness, nor is it attempting to present a solution for the problem of a societal system that provides different degrees of access based on economic status. This book is a tool for police, firefighters, emergency medical technicians (EMTs), paramedics, and others whose job it is to be first on the scene. For easier reading, we will use the umbrella term *first responders* to refer to members of these organizations. Again, this book is a tool, and like any other tool on your belt—your axe, your gun, or your pike pole—pull it out when needed.

Throughout the book you will find mental models, usually in the form of illustrations, that introduce key points. You will see that the first chapters share understanding about the different economic communities and individual behaviors and attitudes within those communities. This is very useful information for first responders working directly with individuals or within different economic communities. As first responders advance in their careers, the job requires them to gain more of a communitywide perspective. The last chapter of this book focuses on how to use this information in a more systemic manner.

I would like to personally thank each of you for what you do! The things you see, the stresses you experience, are at times unspeakable, and yet you do it all over the next day, sometimes the next hour! Though you may not always be told this, know you are appreciated. I hope you find this book to be a useful tool.

–Jodi Pfarr

Key Points

1. This book is written for first responders. First responders are often required to serve economically diverse communities; therefore, the more first-response personnel understand what they are encountering, the less they will react to particular situations—and that means they can better stay in control. Staying in control allows a first responder the luxury of choosing the next action, a choice that ultimately keeps emergency service personnel and the community safe.

2. Communities are diverse in many ways: Age, gender, ethnicity, race, sexual orientation, and economic status, for example, vary by community and within each community. All types of diversity affect communities and should be discussed. This book focuses on economic diversity between and within communities.

3. This book focuses on generational poverty, generational middle class, and generational wealth. Economic classes can be split into many different groups, but if we want to compare/contrast the classes in order to further understand them, using the three categories listed above simplifies our task.

4. This work is based on patterns. All patterns have exceptions. People often choose not to talk about the different ways economic groups operate because they fear being accused of stereotyping. I am not asserting that if you live in one community or the other you are guaranteed to be or act a certain way—that would be absurd. Still, it is equally absurd to state that no differences exist between the different economic communities. We must have the courage to start to talk about the differences in a way that is respectful to all. This book attempts to provide first-response personnel with a better understanding of patterns they witness and experience on the job. This understanding will help first responders keep themselves and the community safer. I trust that first responders will not use the information to profile or

stereotype people but will use it to better understand and relate to the events and people they encounter in their professional capacities. I also hope this book will help readers understand their experience of the societal system at large with regard to economic status.

5. Generational poverty, middle class, and wealth mean that individuals have been in that class for two generations or more. People in a generational class are more likely to exhibit the patterns associated with that class than are people whose families haven't been in it for two generations or more.

6. Situational poverty, middle class, and wealth mean that one spends only a period of one's life in that class. For example, if you grew up in middle class and maintained middle class status into adulthood, but then you experienced poverty due to an illness or other mitigating factor, this would be considered situational poverty. You would not bring the same lenses and mindset to the experience of poverty as would someone who has never experienced anything else.

7. Poverty, middle class, and wealth are all relative. The 2020 Current Population Survey from the U.S. Census Bureau tells us that a household with an annual income of $148,502 or more is in the top 20% of U.S. households as ranked by income,[1] which leads the other 80% of people to consider them rich; however, if you asked households making that amount if they are rich, few would say that they are. They would think of friends who make more money as a basis for comparison. The point is that perception of economic class is relative.

8. Individuals bring with them the hidden rules of the class in which they were raised.

9. Emergency services, schools, social services, and businesses tend to operate from middle class norms and use the hidden rules of middle class. In addition, emergency response as a career creates unique hidden rules for responders that can affect their understanding of other hidden rules.

10. A hidden rule in poverty is that people have to protect themselves against exploitation by other individuals, institutions, and communities. Systems like criminal justice, education, and public assistance do not always treat people in poverty equitably and can sometimes cause harm.

11. In order to move from one economic class to another, an individual must often give up relationships for achievement for a period of time.

12. For first responders to be perceived as good leaders, they must understand the hidden rules in operation and transfer information about laws and policies in a meaningful manner. It is helpful if citizens served by emergency response know the hidden rules of first responders and understand why those hidden rules exist.

13. Again, this book is a tool for police, firefighters, EMTs, paramedics, and others whose job it is to be first on the scene. For easier reading, we will use the umbrella term *first responders* to refer to members of these organizations except in cases where we are talking specifically about any one branch.

Chapter One

Mental Models of Poverty, Middle Class, and Wealth

Mental Models of Poverty, Middle Class, and Wealth

Mental models are pictures, drawings, or stories that communicate a lot of information in a small amount of time. Mental models are frequently used in first response and the military. They not only help deliver a lot of information in a short time, they can also assist in understanding the content. Both police and fire departments use mental models when they train first responders how to be as effective as possible. When a serious crime is committed, the police department will often get a sketch of the person who committed the crime and/or map out the scene. They don't stop at gathering a long, verbal description of the person or crime scene; no, a mental model is created. The mental model helps communicate a lot of information in a short time.

Every one of us already holds mental models of what poverty, middle class, and wealth look like. Some of our mental models of poverty come from our parents or grandparents who to this day save paper bags and rubber bands as a result of their experiences during the Great Depression. Some of us get our mental models of poverty from media. Some of us did not have strong mental models of poverty until we came to work and saw a family in poverty with people working two and three jobs and still barely getting by. Or perhaps the first family in poverty we saw wasn't working at all. Some of us have very strong mental models of poverty because we grew up there. However or wherever we developed our mental models, this chapter attempts to set forth a mental model that incorporates all of the ideas.

Think of an adult in generational poverty (not situational poverty), and follow that adult around for an entire day. What does that person spend time doing? Do the same for a middle class person and a wealthy person.

The circles that follow in this chapter represent average days in the lives of people in poverty, middle class, and wealth. It is worth noting that the mental model used to represent people in poverty was generated by people living in poverty, the middle class circle by people in middle class, and the wealthy circle by someone in wealth. Of course, everybody's circle looks a little different— one item may take up more time in one person's circle than in another's—but the basic components are generally the same.

A Mental Model of Poverty

Let's analyze the circles. We'll begin by looking at the poverty circle. What does transportation look like in poverty? Public transit; walking; bicycling; an older, broken-down car; or, if you have been very successful in an illicit trade, a decked-out ride. Transportation is generally unreliable at best, as is also often the case with housing.

Mental Model of Poverty

Developed by
Philip E. DeVol[2]

Businesses

- Pawn shops
- Liquor stores
- Corner stores
- Rent-to-own
- Laundromats
- Dollar store
- Fast food
- Check cashing
- Temp services
- Payday loans
- Used car lots

The first home address law enforcement receives for someone who lives in poverty is rarely the correct address. A first responder will have to go two or three moves further to catch up with someone. Such things as mental illness and chemical dependency are not always seen in poverty, but any first responder will tell you that they tend to be observed at higher rates overall in poverty than in the other two classes.

Incarceration rates are similar. Not every person from poverty experiences incarceration in the criminal justice system, but go to your local city or county jail or state prison and you'll find that the trend is people from poverty are represented at a higher rate than are those from middle class and at a much higher rate than are people who come from wealth. Why this discrepancy exists is not the focus of this book, but it is a question worth raising and worthy of further analysis elsewhere.

As we look at the poverty circle, we begin to see that the circle is not always stable and that tasks take a longer time to accomplish. In poverty you take the pile of dirty laundry, gather up the kids, and go down to a Laundromat. At the Laundromat you wash the clothes, watch the kids, and unless you have a lot of money, you rarely get the clothes completely dry. Then you run for the bus but miss it, and it is the last bus of the day, so now you call back to the neighborhood to someone who has a car. Remember, it is the only ride in the neighborhood, so the driver has to drop off four other people before picking you up. Gas prices being what they are, you'd better have some gas money. The ride finally arrives; you load up everything and pull away, only to have the unreliable car stall out at the second stop sign. Tasks take a longer time in poverty.

We begin to see that living in poverty is about survival, about getting today's needs met. When your life is about survival, it quickly becomes about today and now—not next year, not even tomorrow; it is all about today and surviving the moment. This point cannot be emphasized enough. In generational poverty it is all about the right now. There is often no grand future story, no picture of what you look like in the future. More time is spent focusing on surviving the moment, which leaves less time to focus on the future. Therefore, in poverty, you will generally hear less talk about going to college or buying a house (future events) than you will hear in middle class.

First responders have noted that people call 911 for nonemergency medical situations that could have been prevented with earlier treatment or addressed later by making an appointment to see a doctor. But when you are living in the now, you address the pain now. Or you push the pain to the side because, in order to survive, you must focus your attention on more pressing issues. Yes, you may have a toothache, but your brother's kids need to be watched. And yes, the tooth hurts more the next day, but you can't miss your appointment with social services. It isn't until 2 a.m., when you awaken to a throbbing mouth, that you call 911 and get an ambulance to the emergency room.

Police officers, how many times have you arrested people who, once they got to jail, seemed very surprised they were there, even though you had seen them making decisions long ago that would lead to jail? A young man in generational poverty (12–14 years of age) once told me he was "getting the heck out." When I asked him what that looked like, he stared at me. I stared back. It was obvious he had never really thought about, nor had anyone talked to him about, what "getting the heck out" looked like. Eventually he gave me an answer I am pretty sure the media fed him: "I'm gonna be a rock star!"

Although he had a desire for some type of change, he had no future story of what this change would look like. This is where first responders have a rare opportunity and power. I know most days it doesn't feel that way, but do not underestimate the impact you, as a first responder, have on each one of these circles. You can give that child a new future story. I travel the nation and present this information. I continuously have people from generational poverty in my audiences say they never would have "made it out" had it not been for a key relationship with someone. Often that someone is a police officer, teacher, firefighter, social worker, or healthcare professional.

When one lacks a strong future story to focus on during a difficult moment, one will often react based on the immediacy of the situation. When a police officer states, "Do this or you go to jail," the reaction is often, "So what?" When one's life is all about right now, that statement is of little consequence; however, when one is focused on the future, as many middle class people are, then one will process that statement in terms of the future. As in, "Wait a minute. If I don't do this, I go to jail. That means the neighbors see me get arrested, and my partner or spouse has to bail me out, and then I have to deal with a lawyer…" The future ramifications outweigh the moment at hand. We will talk more about this concept in the next chapter. The piece to note for now is that because people in poverty are busy trying to survive, life often becomes about the right now, not a future story.

Obtaining Assistance

In the poverty circle, "agency time" refers to the time one spends at different agencies and organizations obtaining various forms of assistance with surviving. In many communities, social service, educational, criminal justice, and healthcare organizations do not work closely with one another, even though many or all of the organizations may be working with the same family. This bureaucratic, compartmentalized way of doing things often has people in poverty running from one place to another to receive services. When the organizations do not work together, it can actually encourage individuals to manipulate the system. When a person from poverty encounters the first organization in the morning, that person nods and smiles and gives the answers the organization wants to hear in order to get what is needed to survive and to be allowed to leave. Then that person goes to the next organization in the afternoon and again nods and smiles and gives them the answers they want to hear in order to get what is needed and to be allowed to leave. By the time people get to their third organization of the day, they are done nodding and smiling. They just tell the organization what is wanted, demand it, and then leave. Often these large systems are not set up to hold anyone accountable or to be accountable to any entities other than themselves.

How is a given social service organization set up? Who sits on its board? Who writes its rules? To whom is it accountable? Rarely are first responders, people in poverty, or others who are directly affected by social service organizations being asked for input or to be involved within the organization in a powerful way. Ultimately, in many of our communities, we have created organizations that act like silos with emergency service personnel and people who utilize the services running between them. For this reason, criminal justice, educational, social service, and healthcare organizations must be willing to work much more closely with each other, learn from one another, and be accountable to one another.

A Mental Model of Middle Class

Let us look at the middle class mental model. In middle class you will often see a career instead of a J-O-B. A career is something you want to hold onto for a while, something on which you can build. A career usually provides the middle class household with health benefits, vacation, sick time, and a living wage. A living wage means you're going to be able to get your basic needs met (food, clothing, and housing). In the United States, a living wage is $16.54 per hour for a family of four.[3] Of course, the amount varies depending on where you are and how much it costs to live there.

A living wage is a major contributor to household stability. Your financial needs are met for today, and that frees you up to focus on the future. How far into the future you can focus often depends a great deal upon the amount of disposable income you earn. If your household makes only $2–4 per hour above the living wage, then you might only be planning 2–4 months into the future. If your household is making $10–15 per hour above the living wage, then you may be looking 30 years into the future, planning for your retirement, saving for the kids' future education, or saving for a hobby like a boat or a cabin in a good hunting area.

A career also gives a person an identity that is recognized by society. Go to a middle class party, and once you have a drink in hand—because middle class is often concerned that you have one—what is one of the first questions people ask?

Mental Model of Middle Class

Developed by Philip E. DeVol[4]

Businesses

- Shopping/strip malls
- Bookstores
- Banks
- Fitness centers
- Veterinary clinics
- Office complexes
- Coffee shops
- Restaurants/bars
- Golf courses

'What Do You Do?'

If you say, "I am a firefighter (paramedic, EMT, police officer, etc.)," people often respond with, "Oh, that must be so rewarding," or, "I could never do that," or, "Hey, I got a ticket the other day. Can you…?" In a later chapter we will discuss family patterns and analyze how having an identity that society at large acknowledges affects parenting.

Transportation

Middle class transportation is generally reliable—you find SUVs, minivans, etc., and sometimes one household will have multiple vehicles. As we analyze the middle class and poverty circles, we begin to see how things like transportation affect daily life. In middle class, people jump into cars that will definitely start, drive to the grocery store, don't worry that they won't be able to afford groceries (their careers' livable wages in most cases guarantee that the money is in a checking account), purchase their groceries, put them into the reliable vehicles, and head home again. In middle class, one's basic needs are usually met, so time and energy are given to other activities. One may choose to get involved with a union, go back to school, pick up a new (or another) hobby, get the kids involved in various activities, or get politically active. The point is that financial resources can help bring stability to the circle. This financial stability is a major element that contributes to one's ability to have a strong future story. It can also help one to contain life's problems so that they don't have an impact on other aspects of one's life.

When transportation is lost in middle class, meaning a vehicle breaks down or is damaged in an accident, the owner of the vehicle often has access to credit. A person in middle class whose vehicle is out of service takes a credit card to the car rental agency and rents a car until the first one can be repaired or replaced. A middle class person may have a relationship with another person who also lives in a financially stable circle. If a neighbor has three cars, people in middle class may be able to borrow one until they can reestablish their own transportation. Thus, the problem of losing one's transportation is contained to just that area of the circle—transportation.

In contrast, people in poverty often do not have access to credit, nor do they have family and friends in financially stable places. Consequently, in poverty, when transportation is lost, the next thing affected is your job. Though you try to catch rides to work, you end up being late one too many times and lose the job. If the job is lost, housing is the next thing that falls into jeopardy. This is how, in the absence of certain resources, one of life's problems can quickly expand to affect numerous other areas of one's life.

It should be noted that as this book is being written, many middle class families are feeling their financial stability slipping away. Due to the rising cost of living, many middle class families are finding it harder to maintain stability within the circle.

A Mental Model of Wealth

In the wealthy circle, your family was financially secure when you were born into it, or you've made so much money in your lifetime that your circle and your children's circle, maybe even your grandchildren's circle, are financially secure. Here it is neither about a J-O-B nor a career; in the wealthy circle, the focus is on managing the money you have, ensuring that your money generates more money, and keeping up connections with others that will assist you in maintaining the status you currently hold.

In wealth, life's problems are not only contained, they are often dealt with by other people. Financial resources are available to compensate people who ensure your basic needs are met. In other words, you have people whose job it is to make sure you are taken care of. People from wealth may sometimes relate to first responders in the same way they relate to their hired help. In their view, first responders are there to assist them with getting their needs met and nothing else.

Mental Model of Wealth

Developed by
Ruby K. Payne[5]

Businesses

- Spas
- Private clubs
- Golf courses
- Plastic surgery
- Concierge services
- Pet spas
- Luxury car lots
- Personal shoppers
- Boutique shopping areas
- Private schools
- Personal security
- Florists
- Party planners
- Upscale hotels
- Private airports with charter and corporate jets
- Upscale travel offices

When responding to calls, first responders will encounter people from poverty, middle class, and wealth. Knowing the hidden rules of each of these classes and applying them in the appropriate situations is essential for gaining mutual respect and trust.

Mental Model of First Responders

First responders have their own driving forces connected to their professions. Ask a responder this question: "What is the definition of a good day at work for you?"

Answer: "Going home safe."

Overwhelmingly, the concept of a call to duty—which includes surviving the day without being injured—has become the priority in emergency response. This driving force affects the same elements identified in other economic classes but with the overriding concept of duty, safety, and self-protection. As a result, a typical day in the life of a first responder will appear much like the graphic below.

Created by
Angel Tucker

Recognizing the different interpretation of each of the elements above, along with the unique nature of some others, provides both responders and citizens a greater sense of understanding of each other.

The response for service from a fire department transcends economic class. Firefighters answer calls to fire emergencies in under-resourced, middle class, and wealthy neighborhoods. But the reception and expectations may be considerably different in each of those environments.

A fire captain once had a complaint filed against his entire platoon because they entered the home of a well-to-do politician and tracked mud onto the carpet with their boots. Fire and medical personnel were responding as they should, to save a life in an emergency regardless of outdoor conditions, but once the crisis was over, the lasting impression in the mind of the homeowner was the messy boot prints all over the floor—after they had been asked politely to take off their boots before entering! In this case, the call to duty is one driving force in conflict with the expectations of a wealthy citizen. While life-or-death situations will always take precedence, it is worth noting that what seems to be an emergency as defined by the responder may not always be considered such by the citizen. In some cases, people in wealth do not see emergency responders as professionals in the same way they see attorneys, tax accountants, and political leaders. Having connections with frontline responders is not seen as necessary in the daily lives of some wealthy people.

People in poverty have a different concept of emergency responders. Many people in poverty see responders almost daily in some form or fashion or are in contact with the criminal justice system. Yet this familiarity does not equate to a singular or agreed-upon interpretation of who the responders are, what their role is, and how important the relationships are to those same citizens.

Persons in poverty are disproportionately frequent consumers of emergency services compared to those in middle class or wealth. People in poverty call police for a number of reasons that are rare among other economic classes. Issues such as mental health crises, civil disputes between landlords and tenants, and zoning and environmental challenges are the responsibility of law enforcement and city government. Persons in middle class and wealth have other options and resources for dealing with these same challenges if such challenges arise at all.

Middle class families tend to view first responders through a broader lens. On one hand, the perception is one of achievement and respect. Most people in middle class respect the work ethic and professionalism of first responders. On the other hand, middle class households tend to be more casual in their interactions with first responders. They may also view certain situations as emergencies that first responders would not. For example, in a middle class community it might be considered appropriate to contact the police to report a neighbor blowing their grass clippings onto the sidewalk. Upon arrival, the first responder would be expected to address the situation with authority. First responders usually live in middle class neighborhoods. This creates a familiarity between responders and the other community members. The familiarity creates a level of comfort, and it is that level of comfort that allows middle class residents to call first responders for situations that are not necessarily emergencies.

The question we ask is this: Since persons in poverty are far and away larger consumers of emergency response efforts, are the results of those services the same as the services provided to middle class and wealthy communities?

Applications in First Response

First responders do not have the luxury of choosing who they want to work with. They are expected to be successful with all citizens. Thus, the more first responders understand about the people they encounter, the more effective they can be. *Be careful here not to confuse understanding with justifying or promoting.* This book does not attempt to justify or endorse any particular behaviors observed in wealth, middle class, or poverty. The hope is that the book will share an understanding that enables first responders to choose their responses carefully and avoid reactionary responses to unfamiliar situations. If one has a reactionary response, it is often perceived as a judgmental response. After all, it is human nature to judge something that is not understood. When first responders are perceived as being judgmental, they quickly find themselves with uncooperative civilians. To understand—not to justify or to promote, but to understand—is the first step toward choosing each of your responses. The ability to choose means first responders stay in control, which builds relationships with civilians, which in turn keeps the first responders safer and makes the job easier.

As we look further into the mental models, we see that the businesses in the communities are different. Businesses present in poverty are focused on survival: pawn shops, check cashing and payday loans, rent-to-own, Laundromats, etc. In middle class, the stores tend to be more specific and sell things that appeal to people whose outlook is future-based: real estate agencies, jewelry stores, antique shops, insurance agencies, travel agencies, and so on. If we recall that a livable wage contributes to a more stabilized circle, we must then ask, "Does the community offer as many livable wage jobs as there are people in poverty?" If people in poverty cannot access jobs in the community that pay a livable wage, chances are that poverty will grow. This directly affects first responders and their departments.

Driving Forces

Another element that has a direct impact on relations between first responders and members of the different communities is the primary driving force in each community. In poverty the driving force is relationships; in middle class it is achievement; in wealth it is connections; in emergency response it is the call to duty and the lawfully mandated responsibilities of the profession.

Relationships

When your world is about surviving, you need other people to help you survive; therefore, relationships affect everything in the poverty circle. This is why the word is written in the middle of the circle. Most law enforcement workers have stories about people who would not provide police with information about another person because of their relationship to that person. The person unwilling to talk would rather go to jail than "rat out" or "snitch on" a friend. Law enforcement personnel who have relationships with people in poverty can attest to the huge advantage those relationships lend to gathering evidence, getting citizens to cooperate, and ultimately keeping one safe and successful, whether transferring someone or solving a crime.

For example, when paramedics deal with "frequent flyers" respectfully, the transport is generally less eventful and stressful. Likewise, consider a police officer who has worked in the same community for more than 20 years, who always treats people in poverty with respect, who holds them accountable in a respectful manner, who takes the time to gain trust through relationships, and who has great moments of success because of it. When this officer goes to a house and explains to a mother that her son is wanted and simply states, "Mrs. Olson, you know me. I promise I will treat your boy well if you turn him over to me. If I have to call for backup, or if another officer has to take him in, I can't promise that," Mrs. Olson calls for her son and tells him to go with the officer. The badge itself doesn't necessarily get you respect in a neighborhood in poverty; relationships will.

TOOL

Power in poverty ≠ the badge, uniform, or title

Relationships in poverty = power and respect

Power and respect = more cooperative citizens and increased personal safety

Once you understand the importance of relationships, you can use them to control your scene. A paramedic was working on a woman known as Mama; the family was very distraught, and the young sons started to yell, pace, and get irritated. A firefighter tried to step in front of them and tell them to settle down, but this quickly increased the frustration and anger. The paramedic interrupted them, saying, "Hey, guys! I need your help! I know you love Mama, so one of you go get the door propped open and the couch moved. The other come here and help me." Giving them a task so they could help their loved one brought the scene back under control.

Building and maintaining relationships can help you as a first responder stay safe and be effective; it can also help the members of your team. You can enter a neighborhood in poverty in a disrespectful manner and survive—it is done daily. But what if a fellow first responder has to return to the same house on the next shift? What kind of treatment will your colleague receive now that the person in poverty personally associates the uniform with disrespect?

A relationship of mutual respect does not mean a first responder has to "kiss ass" or "be nicer" in one neighborhood but not in another. A relationship of mutual respect begins with simply understanding the community you are in and conducting yourself based on that understanding rather than upon judgment. For example, if a wealthy person comes to a middle class party, looks disgusted at the quality of the food and beverages, and is frustrated with the lack of waitstaff, many middle class people at the party will take offense to that response. Why? Because the wealthy person was not operating out of an understanding of how a middle class party works; rather, the wealthy person made a judgment based only upon their experience of how a party should be and acted on that judgment. People don't want others from a different class to tell them their class is inferior. This is as true in middle class as it is in poverty and in wealth. Similarly, a first responder from middle class who enters a situation in poverty and responds judgmentally will also receive a negative reaction. Perhaps you have found yourself in a situation like this on the job, a situation in which you accidentally offended people because you didn't share the same hidden rules. Situations like this are easier to avoid if first responders build their understanding of the patterns of the different economic classes—beginning with the patterns of their own economic class.

Achievement

People in middle class are interested in maintaining stability and hope to gain more stability in the future. As a result, achievement is highly valued. In middle class, if you buy a small starter home and eight years later buy a bigger house, you congratulate yourself. Go back to school and earn a degree? Great! Your favorite team takes it all the way and wins? What could be better? Middle class loves achievement.

On the other hand, a firefighter was installing a smoke detector in a home located in a poverty-stricken neighborhood. When he asked the resident if she owned or rented the home, because the fire department form requires it, she immediately said, "Me? Own this?!" The firefighter thought that he had offended her because of the way she responded. He thought maybe she was there because of current circumstances and wanted him to know that she was better than this rundown place. As he talked to her, he soon realized that she could not conceive of being privileged enough to own a home, even one as neglected and unsightly as the one they were in, and that was the real reason for her response.

Within the United States there are some communities and cultures that absolutely nurture relationships more than other communities and cultures. First responders have noted as they work in many different communities and across many different cultures that some will "take care of each other" more than other communities and cultures. If middle class people feel they live in a community that cares for its members very deeply, or they are from a culture that emphasizes relationships more than others, then they will want to write RELATIONSHIPS right next to ACHIEVEMENT in the circle. However, people who value relationships and achievement equally will spend a lifetime learning to balance the two driving forces.

People will always give back to their communities and cultures, but rarely do they allow that community or culture to overtake the stability of the circle. This balancing can take a lot of time and energy. For example, should you allow people to stay at your house? Sure! As one who understands the importance of relationships, that is something that is expected. But allowing too many people to stay in your house can put the quality of life in the home—and even the housing itself—in jeopardy, which is unacceptable because it disrupts the stability of your circle and undercuts your ability to achieve more in the future.

In generational poverty, no matter the region or culture, relationships are dominant. For example, in poverty you may hear something like this: "What do you mean you can't watch my kids tonight because you have to study for a GED test? I've watched your kids a hundred times!" This is a relationship-based perspective that does not take into account other driving forces—the desire to achieve a passing score on the GED, for example. But, if relationships are dominant, that person is likely to put down the books for the GED and watch the kids.

A high number of emergency responders are recruited from middle class. Agencies want people who have already established a record of lawful obedience, academic success, and financial stability. While responders' primary driving force is a call to duty, the fact that most are recruited from middle class means they also are driven by achievement. Emergency response agencies offer many of the ideals associated with middle class, such as promotion, special assignments, retirement, and community involvement.

As a result, we have a high number of persons from middle class working in emergency response, where the majority of consumers are from poverty, particularly generational poverty. Is it any wonder then that many emergency responders have difficulty connecting with persons in poverty, where relationships are prized?

Law enforcement agencies typically allow seniority to determine assignments and working conditions. High crime areas and the times of day when the most calls for service are handled are usually staffed by personnel with the least amount of seniority. Would it make sense that there would be a higher propensity for failed relationships and for conflict resolution skills to be diminished when the least-experienced personnel are working with people in poverty?

What does this do to the need for developing relationships with the persons in poverty who, again, are our highest level of consumer?

We often see frontline responders who have established important and meaningful relationships with persons living in poverty moved to desk jobs, other locations in the agency, or other areas of the community. Promotions, transfers, and reassignments make it more difficult to create and then maintain relationships.

Connections

In wealth, political, social, and financial connections are essential to maintaining one's status. "Knowing the right people" can in fact ensure that your family's status is maintained for generations to come. Many police officers have stories about pulling over an extremely wealthy person and being scolded, as in, "Do you know who I am? Do you know who I know?"

A police department once participated in a local charity event by having a fake jail and "arresting" people. Then others in the community could make a donation to the cause and release their friends who had been arrested. The department approached a man from generational wealth and asked if he would participate. He hesitated but agreed on the condition that the chief of police be the "arresting officer." Just as people in poverty rely heavily on relationships to survive, and people in middle class rely heavily on achievement to maintain stability, people in wealth rely on political, social, and financial connections to maintain their wealth and social status.

The mental models we have discussed are intended to further our understanding of patterns that first responders observe on the job. In order to truly deepen that understanding, we have to be honest and talk about what we have seen, whether it is "politically correct" or not. We must also be willing to admit that, like all humans, we tend to judge things we don't understand. But this kind of judgment, without seeking first to understand, can make for a long and stressful career. We must have the courage to discuss class in an honest manner, without pulling punches, while maintaining the level of professionalism and respect for the people we serve that the uniform represents. If we do not gain understanding, we will act based on uninformed judgments. That not only puts first responders at risk, it also destroys the potential for learning on both sides of the encounter.

Once, while I was presenting this material to a large group, a person asked me, "When I do a home visit in poverty, every once in a while there is a $75,000 Lexus in the driveway. Can you help me understand that?" If we look back at the mental models, the answer to that question becomes clearer. If you obtain reliable transportation in poverty, does your status in the community increase or decrease? Tenfold, it increases, especially with a luxury car! Being able to provide transportation in poverty is a valuable bartering tool. Perhaps you haven't established a relationship with that person in the community who fixes plumbing. Well, now if your plumbing breaks, you can get it fixed, because there will come a time when the plumber and their family will need a ride. In poverty, repair services are often unaffordable, so you must know how to do it yourself, have a relationship with someone who knows, or have something like transportation to barter.

After hearing that example, another audience member will usually ask, "But isn't there a good chance that the expensive transportation will be lost or destroyed?" When one has a strong future story, that is certainly a concern. However, when you are living for this moment and that expensive transportation causes your status in the community to increase, you are getting more needs met, your family has reliable transportation for the now, and it is worthwhile. Someone else once asked, "Okay, why not get the $6,000 reliable transportation? Why the $75,000 car?"

I responded, "Think of the American dream as a pie; it consists of different slices. In generational poverty, some of our communities are starting to let go of some of those slices. Housing? Probably not going to get it unless someone passes it down. Education? Some communities are starting to let it go. Transportation is one of the slices of the American dream you can still get. Why not put whipped cream and strawberries on that slice? Things are very different in middle class. People in middle class still want, and believe they can achieve, many of those slices: education, vacation, transportation, career, etc. So the prevailing wisdom is that you don't put whipped cream and strawberries on just one slice because that may hinder you from achieving the other slices in the future."

A professor from a major university heard this and said, "Okay, I understand the $75,000 vehicle. I understand why that and not a $6,000 vehicle. But this is what I don't understand: Why not focus your attention on the education slice of the pie? Why not put aside the transportation slice and focus on education, something that can pay off for you in the future?"

The key word there was *future*. Though there are numerous reasons, the biggest is that education is future-based; it does not necessarily help with the right now. Another reason is that you often need finances, time, and transportation in order to further your education, and so you have to work to secure those slices first. Some people in the community may support you in furthering your education, but there will also be those who will challenge you and ask, "Who do you think you are?" The payoffs of education are not immediately visible. If I drive through the community in an extremely nice car, that gets noticed. If I drive through the community with my master's degree, it is not as noticeable; it could even attract negative comments and criticism.

Housing

Many factors within the community directly affect first responders. Still, it is common for communities to point the finger at only one part of the system and blame it for all of the community's problems. We point at the school system and say things like, "If you just learned to teach better, we would not have these low test scores."

To police we say, "If you did your job better, we wouldn't have these increasing crime rates." To social services we say, "If you just did what we pay you for, we wouldn't have poverty in the first place." And so on.

Floor Plan of the House

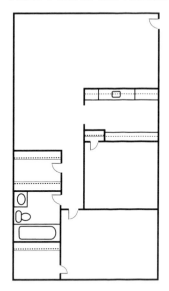

While it is true that all professions should continue to strive to be as effective as they can be, we must also look at other factors in the community that directly affect our jobs. To the right is the floor plan of a two-bedroom house. Envision that two-bedroom house in the generational poverty neighborhood. How many people tend to live there? What do things tend to look like? How does this affect the community? How does it directly affect your job? Now imagine a two-bedroom house in a generational middle class neighborhood. How many people tend to live there? How do things tend to look? How does this affect the community? How does this directly affect your job? Finally, imagine a two-bedroom house in wealth. How many people tend to live there? What do things tend to look like? Is it a main residence, a vacation home, or perhaps servants' quarters? How does this affect the community? How does it affect your job?

It should be noted that in all of these exercises I am asking for what things "tend to look like." Please keep in mind Key Point 4 from the Introduction regarding naming general patterns as opposed to making generalizations.

Criminological research shows that the more non-blood relatives who live in a house, the higher the chances of physical and sexual abuse occurring in that house. The housing situation in your community absolutely affects your job. If someone in your community works full-time and earns $7.25 per hour, that person makes about $1,200 per month before taxes. If that person spends 35% of their monthly income on housing (a standard banker's recommendation to people in middle class), then that person can afford to spend $420 per month on a place to live. A $420 per month budget means that most of the available housing is unaffordable; consequently, people in poverty often share living space. There is no question that this affects the jobs of first responders.

Another crucial difference dictated by the environment at home can be illustrated like this: In middle class, when a coworker is driving you crazy or citizens are simply getting on your last nerve, you often have access to various forms of relief from the situation. In the moment of the other person testing your patience, you may be able to look at that person and think, "In two weeks I go on vacation!" A future story may pull you through the moment. Or, because you have a good housing situation, you might go home to a quiet room and get on the computer, get a drink from the refrigerator, watch TV, take a hot bubble bath, pick up a tool in the garage, or put on the gloves and work the heavy bag to beat some tension out. The point is that in middle class the house is often conducive to taking a break. One may have to wait for the kids to go to bed before it is truly conducive, but usually, at some point in the evening, it is.

Dealing with frustrating people, of course, is not unique to middle class. In poverty you might have a coworker or a social worker who is driving you crazy, and you want the same thing anyone wants—to take a break. But because there are often many occupants, houses in poverty aren't very relaxing places to take a break. For example, you don't want to lock the bathroom door for more than five minutes because someone will need to use the bathroom soon and will start banging on the door. In poverty all the physical space is needed and/or occupied by many people, so other methods of creating personal space are used. Entertainment with an audio component is a popular option. Many kids will come home and put on a headset blaring loudly to drown out everything and everyone else in the house. Adults will put the music up loud or become absorbed in a movie or TV show. Using entertainment to escape is one way to create a break for oneself in poverty, since the busy environment of the house is not conducive. Often there is no future story with a vacation in it, so one gets through the tyranny of the moment by escaping into entertainment. First responders and social workers often ask about the shelves full of DVDs sometimes seen in households in poverty. Those purchases are similar to the purchases people in middle class make at places like Bath & Body Works, Best Buy, etc. All of these personal comfort and entertainment purchases give one a "break," a sense of escape. In poverty there is rarely a big vacation to Hawaii, but one can escape through a movie. Such substances as food, tobacco, alcohol, and illegal drugs can also provide a sense of relief, break, or escape from the moment.

Conclusion

In this chapter we analyzed mental models of generational poverty, middle class, wealth, and emergency responders. We saw that the circles look different, contain different businesses, and are populated by people with different views and patterns. The driving forces for each group must be recognized in order to effectively communicate and establish meaningful dialogue.

We noted that the driving forces for poverty include survival, relationships, and entertainment. Interestingly, emergency responders are also driven by survival, and they acknowledge the need for relationships to be established with the communities they serve. Because responders and persons in poverty share these driving forces, we should promote the fact that these two groups have a great deal in common. Realizing there is common ground for these two groups helps to de-escalate conflict.

As discussed earlier, responders are generally recruited from middle class. As a result, it is important for responders to acknowledge that their preconceptions of others within the different economic classes will not necessarily be consistent with their experiences. We each bring the baggage of our own experiences to every encounter.

Emergency response is a hard job because one must find ways to work effectively with every community. Affordable housing and access to livable wage jobs are just two of many factors that directly affect communities and thus affect first responders' jobs. The better first responders are able to understand the hard things they must witness in all three communities, the better they can stay in control. This control allows a first responder to choose the next move—a much safer option than reacting to a situation without understanding it. Emergency service personnel have to hold each member of each community accountable. The more first responders understand about each of the three communities we discuss in this book, and the better they understand themselves, the more effective they can be in serving all citizens. Consequently, as citizens understand the demands of emergency response as a profession and the driving forces for police, firefighters, and medical personnel, there is a higher probability of establishing effective relationships.

Chapter Two

Hidden Rules

Hidden rules are the rules by which groups operate without ever clearly stating that the rules exist. Different regions, age groups, genders, and countries operate according to different sets of hidden rules. The hidden rules of economic class were first identified by Ruby Payne in her book *A Framework for Understanding Poverty.* In the United States, the South has different hidden rules than the North, the East Coast operates differently than the West Coast, and the mainland is different than the islands. I recall the first time I traveled to the Hawaiian Islands for work; upon deplaning, I was immediately hugged and kissed. This is contrary to the hidden rules of the Midwest, where one hidden rule is that you don't hug and kiss strangers!

The table on the next two pages is from *A Framework for Understanding Poverty.* It describes the hidden rules surrounding many common issues in poverty, middle class, and wealth.

Hidden Rules of Class

	Poverty
Possessions	People
Money	To be used, spent
Personality	Is for entertainment; sense of humor is highly valued
Social emphasis	Social inclusion of people who are liked
Food	Key question: Did you have enough? Quantity important
Clothing	Valued for individual style and expression of personality
Time	Present most important; decisions made for moment based on feelings or survival
Education	Valued and revered as abstract but not as reality
Destiny	Believes in fate; cannot do much to mitigate chance
Language	Casual register; language is about survival
Family structure	Tends to be matriarchal
Worldview	Sees world in terms of local setting
Love	Love and acceptance conditional, based on whether individual is liked
Driving forces	Survival, relationships, entertainment
Humor	About people and sex

Source: *A Framework for Understanding Poverty*[6]

Middle Class	Wealth
Things	One-of-a-kind objects, legacies, pedigrees
To be managed	To be conserved, invested
Is for acquisition and stability; achievement is highly valued	Is for connections; financial, political, and social connections are highly valued
Emphasis is on self-governance and self-sufficiency	Emphasis is on social exclusion
Key question: Did you like it? Quality important	Key question: Was it presented well? Presentation important
Valued for its quality and acceptance into norm of middle class; label important	Valued for its artistic sense and expression; designer important
Future most important; decisions made against future ramifications	Traditions and history most important; decisions made partially on basis of tradition and decorum
Crucial for climbing success ladder and making money	Necessary tradition for making and maintaining connections
Believes in choice; can change future with good choices now	*Noblesse oblige*
Formal register; language is about negotiation	Formal register; language is about networking
Tends to be patriarchal	Depends on who has the money
Sees world in terms of national setting	Sees world in terms of international view
Love and acceptance conditional and based largely on achievement	Love and acceptance conditional and related to social standing and connections
Work, achievement	Financial, political, and social connections
About situations	About social *faux pas*

The unspoken cues or habits of a group are often revealed when someone from outside the group moves in or when someone from the group moves out. In small, rural churches there are many hidden rules in play. One is that certain families have their own pews, so you shouldn't sit there. Members of the congregation might not even realize that there is a rule in play until a visitor to the church sits down smack-dab in the middle of the Johnson family's pew. Only when a hidden rule is broken do we become conscious of the rule itself. Some important hidden rules of which first responders should be aware are listed in the chart on the previous pages. These hidden rules are based on economic class.

A firefighter told me this story:

> When I volunteered to work for the Federal Emergency Management Agency (FEMA) in the aftermath of Hurricane Katrina, my team and I (all firefighters) were sent to a FEMA base camp at Stennis Space Center in Hancock County, Mississippi. During our briefing we were advised not to wear the FEMA shirts that we were issued but to wear our fire department T-shirts instead. People saw FEMA as a large, faceless government agency that they had no relationship with. People of all classes generally trust firefighters. By just wearing our fire department T-shirts, we used this hidden rule to gain social capital with the people we were there to help, and it worked. People were extremely receptive to us when they saw us as firefighters first. Building on that relationship, we were then able to successfully share with them what FEMA aid and programs they were eligible for.

Because first responders will come into contact with all economic groups, it will assist them a great deal if they understand the hidden rules used by the people they are serving. With understanding comes the ability to know your surroundings and choose the behavior you feel will be most successful. Once we learn to identify the hidden rules in play within different economic communities, we must then be willing to understand the hidden rules of different age groups, ethnic groups, and genders, to name a few.

Food

Police officers working off-duty positions at grocery stores often ask about hidden rules regarding food. They say things like, "I don't care if someone is working for their money or receiving welfare; when it is payday, I see folks in generational poverty come in and buy tons of groceries. Even things like steaks and shrimp. How is it that this same family has no food in the house when we visit them on a call two days later?"

Because life in poverty is about survival, you don't always know when you're going to be able to eat. So, one of the hidden rules about food in poverty is that when you have it, have a lot of it. You use food to celebrate, to make yourself feel better, and, of course, you share it with the people with whom you have relationships. If you ever go to a party in poverty, there will be more food than you know what to do with. It is expected that you will stuff yourself at this party and take a plate home. The question of concern is, "Did you get enough?" The point is that when you are fortunate enough to be able to eat, you eat a lot, and you worry about tomorrow when it comes.

People in middle class generally know that they are going to have food available later, so the question becomes, "Did the food taste good?" The emphasis is on the quality. People in middle class will eat for taste and for nutritional reasons. When first responders are on a call in a middle class neighborhood, the cupboards often have food in them. Basic staples like sugar, rice, flour, seasonings, etc. are generally present. A hidden rule about food in middle class is that you keep the basics around because you want to be ready to cook the next meal.

In Chapter 1 we started to think about other factors in the community that affect first responders. The lack of access to healthy food in a poverty neighborhood is one of these factors. For just under $5 you can buy 2,000 calories' worth of food at a fast food restaurant or corner store. This leads to higher obesity rates and other health-related issues that paramedics and firefighters often have to address.

Another factor is that people in poverty sometimes hoard food. When you don't know where you will be staying tonight or tomorrow, when you don't know who will be present to provide for your needs, and when you are pretty sure there is no food where you are staying, you hoard food whenever you get a chance. Under-resourced students regularly hoard food to take home from school cafeterias, taking much more than they can eat in one sitting and stashing it to eat later. Children of divorced parents often hoard food from one parent's home if food is not readily available at the other parent's.

During times when students are suspended from school, the school consequences clearly state that the suspended student is not to return to school property until the suspension is over—but many do. Why? They know there is a place at school that has food, it is the only consistent food source available, and it is usually free. For these reasons, we see many students trespass or sneak back onto school property in order to obtain food, knowing full well that if they are caught, they will be in bigger trouble than before. Hunger can be a powerful incentive for actions many deem criminal.

Power

In middle class, power and respect can be separated. A middle class worker might state, "I don't like my supervisor. Truth be told, I don't even respect my supervisor. But my supervisor is the supervisor, and I respect the power that comes with that position; therefore, I follow my supervisor's instructions."

In poverty, power and respect are directly linked. If a worker in poverty does not respect a supervisor, then that worker may find it extremely difficult to take direction from that supervisor. In poverty, because your survival depends upon other people, it is hard to grant power to those for whom you have no respect. A badge or a title bestowed by an institution does not necessarily get one immediate respect from people in poverty. Relationships are the key to building respect in poverty, and that respect can be translated into power. Developing a relationship will enable an appropriate exchange of power and respect to take place; appealing to a title or to authority will not. This concept affects departments a great deal.

Recall this tool from Chapter 1:

TOOL

Power in poverty ≠ the badge, uniform, or title

Relationships in poverty = power and respect

Power and respect = more cooperative citizens and increased personal safety

In contrast, people in middle class are concerned with achievement and with sustaining their stabilized circle in the future. Others who hold titles and can affect one's achievement are often viewed as "powerful." They are not always respected, but others afford them the power that comes with their positions. Likewise, in wealth, it is necessary to maintain connections in order to sustain the circle and pass it on to future generations. Those who have the ability to change policy and direction are considered powerful, and people in wealth are taught to seek connections with them for this reason. Let's further investigate how this element can affect the careers of first responders.

Middle class parents will often teach their young children to find a police officer if a strange person approaches them or if they become separated from their parents in public. Likewise, people in middle class may have their children tour the firehouse or drop off a card of thanks in appreciation of the job firefighters do. The hidden rule in middle class is that first responders are helpful and good. People in middle class who have bad experiences with first responders usually head down to the department (which they still view as a good and powerful institution) and file a complaint, sure that the benevolent institution will reprimand its wayward employee.

As you may have experienced in your career, the attitude toward first responders in poverty can be much different. In fact, the department often represents just one more institution that tells people in poverty what to do, and so the institution engenders little trust. Fortunately, relationships of mutual respect are powerful enough to override most of the suspicions someone may have about first responders. In a neighborhood in poverty, you might hear something like, "Nope, even though Officer Jones is a cop, she's cool." This means that even though Officer Jones works for an institution that isn't highly trusted, she is viewed favorably because there is a relationship of mutual respect in place.

First responders, especially police, wield their power somewhat effortlessly in many middle class neighborhoods because of the status their position affords them in those communities. The power to arrest and jail citizens means that law enforcement personnel are in a position of authority that commands respect, and they are often treated with respect by people in middle class. In neighborhoods in poverty, and in those in wealth, your authority by itself can mean very little at times. Your standing within that community, meaning whether or not you are respected, will determine whether or not you are afforded power by the members of that community. The amount of power the members of a community afford you is directly related to the level of cooperation you will receive.

Please note that you feel respected when someone meets your expectations. Each first responder has a personal set of expectations, and all of these sets of expectations vary. This means there are several different definitions of respect that a citizen has to figure out. For example, one police officer may feel it is perfectly acceptable for a citizen to speak to police in what is perceived as a loud voice; however, another officer may find it disrespectful. The citizen is left constantly trying to understand what the officer presently handling the situation views as disrespectful.

Time

In middle class, when your supervisor upsets you, what is your response? Is there a part of you that would like to tell your supervisor off? Why might a person in middle class choose not to tell a supervisor off?

In the heat of the moment, people in middle class might feel the urge to tell the supervisor off. However, people in middle class will quickly, almost unconsciously, start to process the moment in terms of the future, as in, "Okay, if I give the supervisor a piece of my mind, then I could get fired, and then I would have to explain that to my partner/spouse. We wouldn't be able to afford our mortgage, I wouldn't have a good job reference, and then my career would…" In a split second, the person in middle class processes the moment in terms of the future and, in most cases, chooses to remain quiet and let the supervisor finish because doing anything else would be detrimental to the all-important future story.

After the incident, some will talk about the supervisor to coworkers, some will file an official grievance, and still others will go home and process it with a loved one. The point here is that people in middle class often perceive time in three distinct segments—past, present, and future—with the future being most important. People in middle class generally won't tell the boss off because of the future ramifications of doing so. The heat of the moment is often processed with the future in mind. How a given response will play out in the future is the primary mitigating factor for a person in middle class who must choose how to respond.

Many people in poverty work jobs that pay less than a livable wage. If (1) you don't make enough money at your job to meet all your needs, (2) it's relatively easy to get the same kind of job down the road, and (3) you are not indebted to anyone for this particular job, what is your response likely to be when the supervisor does something to upset you? Many people in that situation will tell the supervisor off or simply quit. Why should you keep working a job for a person with whom you don't have a relationship and therefore don't respect when that job doesn't even meet your financial needs? In poverty, time is perceived in terms of surviving the here and now. Often there is no grand future story to consider when choosing how to respond. There is a past to consider, but the past usually gets blended with the present moment. Law enforcement personnel have told me many stories in which they ask a witness in poverty about something that happened that day, and the witness starts the response with a story about an event that happened three months previous. This demonstrates how the past can easily become wrapped up with the present moment.

The perception of time affects law enforcement a great deal. When law enforcement personnel spend the last three minutes at a scene trying to say something meaningful to the people involved so that law enforcement will not have to return, they often say things that are meaningful in terms of the future. For example, "Do this again and you are going to jail," or, "Now, we are clear: If I have to come back here, you will get a $50 ticket." A statement like this tends to be very meaningful to people in middle class because they will process it in terms of the future; the statements imply that the consequences will affect one's achievement, a meaningful thing for people in middle class. In poverty the criminal justice system is often perceived as an unavoidable, though unfortunate, part of the circle. Because people in poverty are focused on surviving today, rather than on the future, they are not worried by the threat of incarceration or a monetary fine, both of which are future events. The information is not processed in a way that makes it meaningful, and it will not garner a change in action.

Translate laws and policies into a meaningful form by basing your information on what the community perceives as meaningful.

For example, restate the two statements above in ways that would be meaningful to people in poverty. It might go something like this: "So, are we clear that if you choose to have Billy monitor the music and keep it low, then you have chosen not to have to see my ugly mug again tonight?" Remember that humor is often appreciated in communities in poverty. You'll want to be sure to continue: "But, if you choose not to have Billy monitor the music, then you have chosen not only to see me again but also to receive a fine. I know a fine might not be a big deal, but if you choose not to pay it, it turns into a warrant, and then three months from now, every time you see a squad car in the neighborhood, you'll be wondering if today's the day they called it in. It's your choice."

As you recall some scenes you've encountered on the job, think of these hidden rules and the information in Chapter 1 to gain further understanding about what you have witnessed. For example, paramedics were called to a house in poverty where an adult male lay on the couch watching a large-screen TV. (Recall that TV can be a form of taking a break, just as a vacation may be to people from middle class or sailing is to the wealthy.) A young woman escorted the paramedics to a bedroom where a middle-aged woman who weighed approximately 600 pounds lay in bed and complained of pain in her buttocks.

The young woman said she would help paramedics get the woman in bed to the ambulance. The paramedics knew they would not be able to transport the woman to the ambulance, so firefighters came to take the front door off the hinges and ensure that the patient could get out. While they did this, the man on the couch yelled, "Don't wreck that door!" Recall that the fire department represents one more of the many agencies in this man's life—agencies he does not trust and does not feel listen to him. So when those agencies enter his space, he may suspect they will treat him and his property differently than they would others.

The woman was successfully transported to the hospital, and the firefighters replaced the door, but many walked away from that scene confused by all they had encountered.

As you reflect on this scene, think about how entertainment and food can be used as escapes; how there is access to cheap, high-calorie, low-nutrition food; how relationships will assist you in the moment to survive; and how departments may be viewed based on the prior "agency time" a person has experienced.

First responders also talk about being called to a middle class neighborhood where a person driving by saw a person lying in the street. When first responders get there, it is a person experiencing homelessness trying to get some sleep. This leads first responders to ask themselves and each other, "If the caller was so concerned, why wouldn't they just get out of the car and check on the person?" In middle class, people are focused on achieving, and maybe this means getting to a function, a meeting, or a child's activity on time, leaving no time to stop and check on a person lying in the street. Also, middle class has great reverence for titles, so a middle class person without a title like "firefighter," "officer," or "EMT" may not feel qualified to address someone in distress or may feel it is the job of that person with the title to deal with it.

Talking About Change

Anyone can ask (or tell) another person to do something different— to change. That does not mean the other person will do it. It is only when something is said in a way that is meaningful that another person will respond in the desired manner. For example, you could tell me to lose weight all day long, but until the information is stated in a manner that is meaningful to me, there is a strong chance that I won't follow your advice. The analogy to emergency response here should be pretty clear. First responders are constantly telling people to modify their behavior and/or actions so emergency service personnel will not have to return to the scene and take further action. Until first responders are able to help people understand that what they are saying is meaningful, their advice falls on deaf ears.

Many law enforcement personnel will say, "But I made it meaningful: I told them that if they do it again, they'll go to jail." Refer back to the mental model of poverty. If you see jail as an unavoidable part of your circle and you are focused solely on the here and now, then you don't perceive jail as a major threat. In middle class, however, because you don't want to be known as the person who went to jail last week, and because you immediately process the fact that being in jail will affect your future achievement, the same threat of incarceration is much more meaningful.

The point is that first responders should not focus solely on telling the truth; rather, they should focus on telling the truth in an effective way. If you told me today that I should lose weight, well, guess what? You're right. I am an intelligent person, and I am fully aware that carrying as much weight as I do on my frame can have some very serious health ramifications. Does that get me any closer to losing weight? No! A hundred people could tell me today that I should lose weight, and each one would be right. But I hope that being right, or that telling me the truth about my weight, keeps all one hundred people warm at night, because it certainly doesn't have the intended effect—i.e., getting me to lose weight. People may have all the information, but it is not until that information becomes meaningful to them that they will be motivated to change.

The ability to make things meaningful to others is what makes strong leaders effective. Perhaps you remember a time when the department made a personnel rule that got passed down to you without explanation and you were told to comply. You didn't understand why they changed the rule, no one asked for your input, and no one explained why this was happening. How did you or how would you feel in a situation like that? Many of us will grumble to each other about that rule, about the management, and about how they have nothing better to do with their time, right? Most people do not respond well to being told they must change. It is much easier to bring about effective, long-term change when individuals themselves identify the problems and suggest future solutions.

A research project published in the *Harvard Business Review* concluded that people in the criminal justice system cared as much about the fairness of the process through which an outcome was produced as they did about the outcome itself. The research project later defined fairness with three major principles: Engagement means involving individuals in the decisions that affect them by asking their input and allowing them to dispute the merits of another's ideas and assumptions. Explanation means that everyone who is involved in and affected by the decision should understand why final decisions are made as they are. Finally, an expectation of clarity requires that once a decision is made, the rules of the game are clearly stated.[7] First responders generally practice these principles. Learning about hidden rules will assist with engagement and setting expectations, and learning how language functions in the three major economic classes will help with explanation.

Remember that almost every service organization is asking the citizen (client, customer, etc.) to change. Whether it is to eat healthier, smoke less, work more, get married, get divorced, be a more active parent, read to one's kids, keep one's music down, get this form to that place, stop fighting, whatever the organization's purpose is, ultimately the organization asks the person it serves to change so that the person receiving service won't need the service in the future. Change has a much better chance of happening when the person being asked to change processes the problem and helps determine what the solution will look like.

When I not only admit that I am overweight but also admit that it is a problem and have enough space to process how it will look to lose the weight, then I stand a much better chance of making a long-term change. Ultimately, as a first responder, do you want to drive home saying, "Well, I told them the truth"—or do you want to drive home saying, "Well, I was effective today"? To be effective doesn't mean that you don't tell the truth; it simply means that you tell the truth in a way that is meaningful and engages the people listening.

Now, if you're feeling like the approach outlined above is too "cute and sensitive" or "touchy feely" to be effective, let's look at how it might work in a first responder's own life. Think of a superior you did not like and didn't even respect. What was your response to this "bad leader"? Not working as hard, talking behind their back, showing less loyalty, and being generally uncooperative are just a few common responses. And when you had superiors you respected, even though you may not have agreed with them all the time, you had respect for them. What was your response to them? Cooperation, hard work, and loyalty are common. The minute you say you work in emergency response, whether you are on the streets or answering the phones, you will be looked upon as a leader.

Whether you want to be a leader or not is somewhat irrelevant; first responders are viewed as, and are expected to be, leaders in the community. If the communities you serve view you as a bad leader, then you should expect many of the responses listed above from the civilians you work with; they will be uncooperative and won't work as hard or give as much as they would if they viewed you as a good leader. One of the quickest ways to get labeled a bad leader is to say things in ways that are not meaningful to the people you are addressing. The tool above is about understanding the communities you work in, which will allow you to make your information meaningful, be viewed as a good leader, and thereby benefit from the positive responses good leaders generate.

Family

Recall from the first chapter that people in middle class often have careers—not just a J-O-B—and that those careers give them an identity that is generally respected by the larger societal system. When one has access to a career, one has access to a different way of forming an identity. In their book *Promises I Can Keep,* Kathryn Edin and Maria Kefalas discuss how this element affects becoming a parent.[8]

Do this exercise: Think of as many women as you can who are older than 23, single, have no children, and who live in middle class. Just think of as many as you can. Now think of as many women as you can who are older than 23, single, have no children, and live in poverty. Again, think of as many as you can. Many readers will be able to think of more women in middle class than in poverty. Why? One of several reasons is that women in middle class have access to many identities that society at large will acknowledge.

"What, young lady, you are going to be a lawyer?" When something like this is heard in middle class, it is often meant in a congratulatory manner, because the title "lawyer" gives one an identity that middle class acknowledges and honors. The young woman in question does not need to be, nor is she expected to have to be, a mother right now, which allows her to try to achieve a career-related identity. She has more than one way to achieve an identity that the societal system will honor. In poverty there is often less access to different kinds of respected identities; however, one identity that is still honored by society at large, and is still accessible, is "parent."

Statistics show us that single parenthood is more prominent in poverty than in other classes. In these cases, the mother is usually the primary parent; therefore, in poverty the matriarch generally has the primary relationship and thus holds much power within the family structure—even in the community at large.

TOOL

Utilize the power the matriarch holds.

In Chapter 1 we discussed a scenario in which it was the mother who ordered her son to go with a police officer. When first responders are called to a house to handle a domestic dispute in poverty, they will do well to look for the matriarch and speak with her. Often a man will step in and try to talk over her. At this point first responders should move their attention to the man who interrupted. If another person involved in this call is on the scene, that person will jump in and interrupt him. There is no way this third person will let the first responders talk only to that guy. Separate these two parties to keep yourself safe, and go back to the matriarch. I have seen matriarchs give a simple nonverbal that told others to step back. Building a relationship of mutual respect with the matriarch not only gives you power in your interactions with her, it also gives you power within the family structure and possibly within the community. Please note that the oldest woman on the scene is not necessarily the matriarch.

Hidden Rules for Emergency Responders

Gary D. Rudick

When I began my law enforcement career, the use of seat belts was not the law, it was just a good idea, and few officers used them. Yes, I know that was back when Henry Ford was first building automobiles, but stay with me.

In the 1970s and early '80s, cars were equipped with seat belts, but most people did not use them. Hard to believe now, isn't it? Cops argued they should not be forced to wear seat belts because, they argued, seat belts restrained their ability to get out of the car quickly as they arrived at the scene of a crime. Exiting a patrol car with gun in hand might be necessary, and the lap and shoulder belts interfered with that necessity. When laws made seat belt use mandatory, cops cheated. We began to use them in lawful compliance, but we privately reserved the right to take them off just before we got to our destination or anytime we felt a quick exit was necessary. We never made this issue public. Over time the practice became one shared with new recruits and across the professional spectrum. It became a hidden rule.

After nearly 35 years of policing, and after being retired for nearly 10 years, I still find myself taking off my seat belt when I get to within about 100 yards of my destination. It drives my wife nuts. She will turn and say, "What are you doing? You planning on jumping out and going in foot pursuit? Put that back on!"

There are tons of hidden rules for emergency responders. Eating at a restaurant? You take the seat near the rear of the establishment, have your back to the wall, and face the main entry doors. Is that taught in police and fire academies? Nope. It is a rule you learn from your peers because you want to be ready if danger enters. Where does your spouse sit in a booth at a restaurant? Inside, always. You may need to exit and take action in an emergency. This is a hidden rule.

Kevin Gilmartin, in his book *Emotional Survival for Law Enforcement,* defines the practice of daily seeking survival and prioritizing safety as a condition known as hypervigilance.

Hypervigilance, according to Gilmartin, is "the necessary manner of viewing the world from a threat-based perspective, having the mindset to see the events unfolding as potentially hazardous."[9]

If your profession requires you to work every day within a threat-based environment, every encounter must be viewed as a potential threat. The idea becomes, "I know not everyone or everything is a threat, but if a threat arises, I've got to be ready." This method of seeing the world from a threat-based perspective is not inconsistent with the survival skills necessary for people existing in poverty. Both first responders and people in poverty have a driving force toward survival on a regular basis.

Earlier we discussed asking first responders the question, "What is a good day for you?" The answer: "Going home safe." In order to survive, responders have some hidden rules that are based on a threat-based perception of the world. When taken to the extreme, this can cause conflict between citizens and police.

I had a police officer tell me that he never shakes hands with any citizen. Shaking hands, he said, left him vulnerable to an attack. The individual could pull him off his feet, pull him down to the ground, and more easily assault or disarm him. As a result, his personnel file was full of complaints from citizens who saw his conduct as aloof, rude, and racist. It never occurred to him how someone of a different race than him would react to the refusal to shake hands. For him, this was an issue of survival.

Likewise, it is well-known in generational poverty that if you intend to survive, if you are determined not to be a victim, you must learn to fight. Gaining a reputation as a fighter reduces the opportunity for others to make you a victim. It also means you must maintain a high degree of hypervigilance in order to know when you may be attacked, where danger resides, and what the threats are in your immediate area. You understand, like an emergency responder, that while not everything is an actual threat to your safety, you must be ready when one presents. If you are not prepared, you may be attacked, you may be injured, or you may be killed.

Officers approach every person they encounter with a certain degree of caution, not knowing exactly who the person is and what they may do. Breathing is accelerated, pulse is rapid, and tunnel vision is enhanced. Hypervigilance is in effect. The potential for a misunderstanding and escalation is clearly present. When a person in poverty is approached by a police officer, many of the same anxieties, fears, and cautions are exhibited by the citizen in this context. People in poverty have to be on alert for harm that may come from other individuals, the community, and even institutions (including the education and criminal justice systems) that have not always treated people in poverty equitably and have sometimes even caused harm. Again, the potential for escalation of conflict is extremely high.

Emergency responders also have hidden rules about humor. Gallows humor is used as a defense mechanism to survive the psychological assault on the brain that results from the stress of the job. Making fun of people, even ridiculing circumstances of death, is done in order to tell yourself "this is not real." You make fun of these terrible things and laugh in order to avoid becoming emotionally attached. This helps to deal with post-traumatic stress disorder (PTSD).[10] Humor is one of the most frequently utilized methods of guarding one's mental health among people who work in such challenging environments.

I have a video of a man in custody who is about to be interviewed for a terrible crime. A detective hands him a bottle of water and leaves. When the detective is out of the room, the suspect takes out a gun, calmly puts it to his head, and pulls the trigger. The detective returns and begins a profanity-laced tirade because no one had searched the individual for a weapon prior to his entry into the room. The video causes anyone who is not an emergency responder to gasp in disbelief, to turn away and become visibly shaken. But for emergency responders? They laugh out loud, much to the shock of people in the room who are not emergency responders. The emergency responders are not laughing because the man is dead. They are laughing at the response of the detective who, in their minds, could be any one of them. It's a ton of paperwork. It will require a host of explanations and excuses. Every responder knows the error could have been their own, and they are thankful that today it is not. This type of dark humor is used to reduce the mental health effects of traumatic experiences.[11]

Consider the use of a bulletproof vest. It is used to protect an individual's body from a fatal threat. Dark humor, in this vernacular, is a bulletproof vest for the brain. If you can laugh at the most terrible things in life and ridicule your own fears, the effects on your emotional state are somewhat reduced. Humor becomes a bulletproof vest to protect your brain from what would otherwise be an injurious experience. Without humor, these terrible experiences may become too much for any one person to endure without resulting in mental health damage. Additionally, displaying humor in the face of danger is a form of bravado. This is what emergency responders as a profession share and use to build esprit de corps. We cannot show fear and instead show humor as a way to reduce the display of a fearful emotion.

This form of humor in the face of tragic events is closely related to the type of humor expressed in generational poverty. It is unique, not shared or valued within middle class or wealth, and is one that people in generational poverty can relate to even though they are not responders. Because a hidden rule in poverty is that you can't stop bad things from happening, people in poverty often use humor as a way to lessen the effects of unfortunate, even tragic, situations.

Finally, we know that emergency responders develop uniquely powerful relationships with each other that transcend most normal relationships in middle class and wealth. The experience of surviving dangerous and even life-or-death encounters creates a bond that is nearly unshakable. Responders will overlook the mistakes of their peers even to the point of covering those mistakes with their own behavior, statements, and testimony. They will gladly risk their own career for that of a coworker. The so-called "thin blue line" is often compared to the "no snitching" mentality of persons in poverty. First responders often think, "We are in this together, and we don't give anyone up. I have your back. You've got mine. We are against everyone else." For both first responders and persons in poverty, relationships are critical for survival. For responders, this hidden rule includes the concept of protecting those you work with as a high priority; they are like family, and your own protection is connected to how well you protect them.

Firefighters and emergency medical personnel often work a shift schedule of 48 hours on and 24 hours off. This schedule means they spend more time at the station and with their coworkers than they do with family and friends. The bonds created here are as strong as any within the family unit and tell us a great deal about why persons in emergency response professions have such a high rate of suicide. After leaving the profession, the feeling of being dissociated and disconnected from the kinds of relationships that have been the norm for decades leaves the individual wanting, not sure of their own identity and craving the emotional stimulus they previously enjoyed. Relationships become a significant component of the career for these professions.

***

Conclusion

The communities that first responders serve look and operate differently from one another. The hidden rules found in each community are different, and we must remember that it is not a matter of which set of hidden rules is "better" than others. No one can justify some of the things first responders see in wealth, middle class, and poverty. Again, the focus should not be on determining which system of hidden rules operates "better" than others; rather, care should be taken to learn to be effective with the people in each economic class you serve. Being effective means not only understanding the community and the people in it but also developing the ability to transfer information in a way that is meaningful to each citizen. When citizens are able to recognize the significance of a law or directive and how it will affect them personally, they are much more likely to obey it. First responders who are able to transfer information in meaningful ways are generally viewed as good leaders, which makes citizens more willing to cooperate with them and ultimately obey laws and regulations. When citizens follow guidelines and laws, it not only proves emergency response personnel effective, it also keeps them safe and makes the job easier.

When we look at the driving forces for economic classes, we see that the primary forces for persons in generational poverty are survival, entertainment, and relationships. These are also driving forces for emergency responders, who desire daily survival, entertainment and humor that help them cope with the stress of the job, and peer relationships that are highly valued since they mature under stress and in the face of challenges. As a result, we see that emergency responders have more in common with persons from generational poverty than they might have imagined. We also see how conflict may escalate when one or both groups believe their own survival is at risk when contact occurs.

The similarities between first responders and people from poverty also allow the possibility of effective dialogue and an exchange of ideas, concerns, fears, and empathy. When we have something in common, we can move forward with more productive conversations. An understanding of the driving forces for emergency responders and for the three economic classes—especially poverty—means a better understanding of how to avoid conflict and how to keep conflict from escalating when it does occur.

Because relationships are key for both first responders and people in poverty, their shared experiences can be used to help build the critical relationships necessary for each group to succeed.

Chapter Three
The Importance of Language

Language is the primary mode of human communication, but not all people who speak the same language speak it in the same way. In a book called *The Five Clocks: A Linguistic Excursion into the Five Styles of English Usage,* Dutch linguist Martin Joos identified five different registers of language that range in usage from very intimate to very public.[12] The register a person uses is often as strong a determinant of the outcome as the actual words being spoken. In fact, using the wrong register in a given situation can lead to misunderstandings, offense, and in some cases (like those involving intimate register used to sexually harass another person), disciplinary and/or legal action.

The following chart identifies each of the five registers and gives descriptions and examples.

Registers of Language

Register	Explanation
Frozen	Language that is always the same. For example: Lord's Prayer, wedding vows, etc.
Formal	The standard sentence syntax and word choice of work and school. Has complete sentences and specific word choice.
Consultative	Formal register when used in conversation. Discourse pattern not quite as direct as formal register.
Casual	Language between friends, characterized by a 400- to 800-word vocabulary. Word choice general and not specific. Conversation dependent on nonverbal assists. Sentence syntax often incomplete.
Intimate	Language between lovers or twins. Language of sexual harassment.

Source: *Bridges Out of Poverty*[13]

Joos showed in his research that these five registers exist in every language. You will hear each register in every region. Different regions of the United States are often associated with particular registers, but these associations are popular misconceptions. All registers of language are found in all regions. For example, when people in the North hear a strong Southern drawl, they may assume the person is speaking in casual register. This assumption may be very inaccurate, as people with strong Southern accents can and do speak in the formal and frozen registers. Activities of the court, lectures at academic institutions, and corporate activities all take place in formal register in the South, and marriages, funerals, and church services are carried out using frozen register.

We see the opposite effect when people from the United States hear a strong British accent—they tend to think that the person is speaking in formal register. However, British people, like everyone else, utilize casual register too. All registers exist in all regions.

How often a person speaks each register varies according to many factors, but to associate one register with a particular accent, region, or country is a false assumption that can easily cause a misunderstanding. And as emergency service personnel well know, a simple misunderstanding has the potential to put a first responder in danger very quickly.

People in generational middle class tend to use formal register more frequently than people in generational poverty. They use words to negotiate, revealing an important point about middle class: There is a strong emphasis on verbal communication and negotiation. People in generational poverty tend to use casual register more often than people in middle class and wealth. Language within casual register tends to be about survival—statements that get you through the moment. Linguistic research tells us that all humans rely on nonverbal signs when communicating; in casual register, the awareness of nonverbal signs is heightened.

Nonverbal Communication

In generational poverty, nonverbal communication (gestures, facial expressions, monosyllabic expressions, etc.) is emphasized. It is an external world; if you want to survive, you'd better feel it, hear it, or see it coming at you. Recall from Chapter 1 the house in generational poverty. There are often many people in one dwelling. When Uncle Fred comes home drunk, one needs to know if Uncle Fred is going to pass out or if he's going to start a fight. Uncle Fred never verbally articulates what he intends to do, but his nonverbals make it clear. Being able to see, feel, and hear nonverbal signals that are sent to you will help you survive in poverty; in fact, this ability is absolutely mandatory. Teachers have reported students in school hitting other students without recognizable provocation. When asked to explain the behavior, the aggressors' most common responses were along the lines of, "Because they were looking at me."

Absolutely! In poverty, if someone gives you a dangerous look, it may be in your best interest to attack preemptively before you yourself are attacked. Because nonverbal cues communicate information, they are being interpreted quickly and are relied upon as heavily as verbal communication. First responders must be conscious of what their nonverbals are communicating. I can't stress this enough: *In a neighborhood in poverty, nonverbal communication is as important as verbal communication.*

Consider this story once shared with me by a judge: The judge was having a difficult time with some of the people over whose cases he presided. More than one defendant had accused him of calling them stupid and being disrespectful toward them. This puzzled the judge because he had never called anyone in his courtroom "stupid," and he always tried hard to conduct himself in a respectful manner. When he asked his mentor about this, the mentor explained to him that his nonverbal gestures were sending that message. The defendants were most likely responding to the judge's negative nonverbal cues. Armed with the understanding that some people are more acutely aware of nonverbal communication than of the words being spoken, the judge returned to his court conscious of monitoring his nonverbals and experienced much greater success.

Developing an acute awareness of nonverbal communication will help first responders on the job. In particular, developing an awareness of—and more importantly, the ability to control—one's own nonverbal cues will prove extremely useful. An easy test is to take a moment to focus on what that little voice in the back of your head is saying. It usually exerts unconscious control over your nonverbals. If you are approached by the same citizen with the same concern three times in one shift, and during these encounters that little voice in the back of your head is saying, "Wow, this person is slow," you will often reflect that sentiment unconsciously with your nonverbals. Though first responders are trained to be professional and will address this person in a polite, professional manner, a first responder's nonverbals may communicate very clearly what the first responder is actually thinking. A person who lives in an environment in which knowing how to read nonverbals is a necessary survival skill will likely notice the message you're sending with your nonverbals. If the message is, "Wow, this person is slow," or something similar, one of two responses is likely: The person will either shut down or confront you and ask something like, "Why are you treating me this way?"

The best example of this comes from police officers who are attempting to interview witnesses from generational poverty. Officers routinely give attention to the radio microphone attached to their uniform shirt, which is usually barking information while the conversation proceeds. When officers give even slight attention to the radio transmissions, this says to the witness that the officer is not interested in what witnesses have to say. When potential witnesses feel unvalued or disrespected, they may cut the conversation short or leave out important details. Because entertainment and storytelling are highly valued by persons in poverty, diminishing or ignoring the person who is speaking is a sign of disrespect you can ill afford to make when attempting to gather important information about a crime. It also undermines any attempt at relationship building.

One of the most intimidating nonverbal acts performed by law enforcement officers is putting their hand on their holstered firearm. This is often nothing more than an effort to rest or stand in a comfortable position. In some cases, it is a gesture meant to affirm an officer knows where their gun is and is ready if there is a need to draw quickly. But for many civilians it is seen as a threat and can escalate conflict. Be mindful of where you are putting your hands in relation to the person you are speaking to, and try to anticipate what they are seeing in your nonverbal actions. Is it possible to rest your forearm or elbow on the firearm rather than your hand when you are already aware there is no threat present? Your nonverbal behavior can send an unintended message that your words will not be capable of overcoming.

Another example comes from a house officer of a fire station. They had an individual who visited the station on a regular basis to get his blood pressure taken. The fire station offered this as a courtesy to the public. After several visits from this particular visitor, some EMTs and paramedics reported that he made inappropriate comments. Not threatening, but inappropriate nonetheless. So, the house officer began coming out to observe when this gentleman would come in to get his blood pressure checked.

The house officer was polite and professional in what he said to the man, but still the visitor started complaining about the house officer. When the house officer read the complaints, they stated several times that the house officer would flex his chest, "swell up like a bull," and purse his lips at the man. When the house officer read this, he realized his nonverbal signals were being perceived as an attack by the visitor even though his words were not aggressive or rude. The next time the man came to get his blood pressure checked, the house officer was intentional about his nonverbals, and the visitor engaged him in conversation.

Language Function: Survival and Negotiation

Within casual register, words are used to survive. When you live in an external world, commands like "Sit down," "Stop it," "Start that," or "Move it" are all the language of survival. They are words that will get you through this moment. They will help you survive. If children are to remain safe, they must follow directions. This is especially important in poverty. When someone yells out, "Get down!" you need to know your child will do so. In that situation, to have a child respond with words of negotiation—"Approximately how far down? And if I choose to get down, do I get a reward?"— will not aid survival; in fact, it can be detrimental. Words of survival ensure the safety of you and your loved ones and are expressed frequently within casual register.

In middle class, words are used to negotiate. Words of negotiation are about bringing meaning to a situation in order to negotiate a behavior. For example, in middle class, parents might yell outside to their child, "Bobbie, come on in." But they know their Bobbie, and he is not coming in the first time he's called. So the middle class parents quickly bring meaning to the situation to negotiate the desired behavior. "Bobbie, come on in or your supper will get cold."

When Bobbie comes in and sits down at the table with filthy, dirty hands, his middle class parents will continue with words of negotiation. "Bobbie, didn't I see you playing under the old oak tree? Yes? Well, isn't that the oak tree that Mr. Johnson's dog always relieves himself on? Do you think your ma wants Mr. Johnson's dog's relief on her food? Please go wash your hands."

Words of negotiation in the formal register were being used with the child the entire time. This gives Bobbie access to the syntax and vocabulary of formal register; it also helps him assign meaning to the world around him. Because middle class is such a verbal world, people in middle class are eager to facilitate their children's verbal skills and thereby help the children understand the world around them. Highly developed verbal skills help children in middle class negotiate, stay safe, and achieve their goals.

Practicing negotiation using formal register teaches many cognitive lessons. Imagine you are a middle class parent who gets a phone call at 1 a.m. from the day care center stating they cannot watch your children today because a water pipe burst. At 1 a.m. there are only two people you can call: your mom and your sister. Your sister already has obligations and can't help you. Your mom agrees to watch the oldest two children but not the youngest. Mom is getting older and cannot handle all three children. It becomes clear to you that you will have to take your 5-year-old daughter with you to the training you are going to attend for work that day.

As a middle class parent, what do you pack for her? Tons of quiet games, toys, and snacks. During the ride to the presentation site, you talk to the 5-year-old about what is coming up (future story) and what the expectations are (understanding the middle class rules in operation). Once you get to the site, you set up the quiet toys and games, set snacks out, and go through the expectations one more time. This time you inform your child that if she is loud, then the nice people around her will not be able to hear; but, if she is quiet, not only will people be able to hear, she will also get a yummy juice bottle at break time. If she starts to get louder, you will remind her that she is in jeopardy of losing the juice bottle.

What cognitive lessons did you nurture during this exchange? Most importantly, you reinforced the concepts of future orientation and sequence by constantly letting the child know what comes next and what the expectations will be. Choice is emphasized by letting the child know that if she chooses to remain quiet, she will get a reward, but if she chooses to be loud, she'll get nothing. Delayed gratification and consequence are also cognitive concepts being indirectly nurtured as a result of using formal language and words of negotiation.

In generational poverty you often wouldn't have time for all of that. In fact, the story might go something more like this: Your sister-in-law didn't show up to watch your children this morning, so you have to run through the neighborhood to find someone to watch them. While you are attempting to do this, the person who was going to give you a ride to work has to leave or she will be late for work. You finally get someone to agree to watch the two older children but not the youngest, so you take her with you. Because your ride left, you have to take the bus, which makes you nearly an hour late to your training site. When you come in the door, the entire audience is swearing at you—not verbally, but their nonverbals tell you very clearly that they are highly frustrated with you. You sit your daughter down and tell her, "Sit down and shut up," and then you pull out your tablet and pen and go to work. You only had time/need for words of survival, for language that would get you through the moment—a definite contrast with middle class and its emphasis on words of explanation and negotiation. A job in emergency response requires one to understand both casual and formal register. While responsibilities like attending community meetings, courtroom appearances, and meetings with supervisors call for formal register and words of negotiation, such duties as directing citizens while on an active crime scene often call for survival-oriented words in casual register. Understanding the different registers and how the different economic groups utilize them gives you more insight into how and why people respond to you in the register of language that they do.

Discourse Patterns and Story Structure

The differences between casual and formal register mentioned above—vocabulary, words of negotiation versus words of survival, and verbal communication versus nonverbal communication—are not the only differences. The discourse patterns also vary. Recall the citizen who was asked about something that happened that day and whose answer started with something that happened three months ago. As you tried to follow this long story of what happened, you probably found it hard to keep track because so many people and so many seemingly unrelated events were mentioned. This is because the two different registers use two different discourse patterns. In formal register the discourse pattern is direct, while in casual register it is circular.

People in middle class use formal register often; therefore, they generally tell a story in a very direct way, starting with the first event and recounting the rest of the events that led to the most recent event. Usually the story builds up to the most important points and then comes down with a concluding sentence or two. In contrast, people in generational poverty tend to use casual register, and the casual register story is told in a circular pattern.

Discourse Pattern

Formal Register Discourse Pattern

Speaker or writer gets straight to the point.

Casual Register Discourse Pattern

Speaker or writer goes around the issue
before finally getting to the point.

Source: *Bridges Out of Poverty*[14]

Story Structure

Formal Register Story Structure

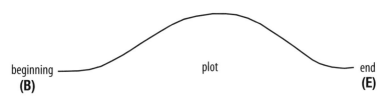

Casual Register Story Structure

Source: *Bridges Out of Poverty*[15]

The graphics above provide mental models of the two different story structures. The formal register story has a clear beginning (B), and the action builds up to the main plot element or the point of the story. Then the action tapers back down to a clear ending (E). Remember this hidden rule about time in middle class: It is viewed in terms of the past, present, and future. For this reason, the story moves chronologically. The point of the story is to share information, so it is designed to cover the necessary elements from the past, make a point regarding the present and/or the future, and let everybody move on. Have you ever been in a middle class community meeting where someone simply fails to make a point and move on? Painful, isn't it? To people who are used to hearing and telling stories that are presented in a clear-cut, chronological structure, a circular story structure does not seem to meet the goal of information sharing.

In generational poverty, because the casual story structure is used, there is no straightforward beginning. A person may start a story by relating something that occurred three months ago or start with an entirely different story they feel is necessary background information—e.g., "I told you that story to tell you this one…"

As the story progresses, there are points at which audience participation is acceptable. At times it is even expected. The small insertion markers in the mental model represent places in the story where, if there is a relationship with the listeners, the listeners are expected to jump in with commentary or share experiences of their own. This casual register story structure is as much about being entertaining as it is about sharing information.

If a person in poverty is telling a first responder a story, and the person is thinking that the first responder is "okay" but for some reason is not participating in the storytelling, the person may give verbal cues or make gestures that indicate the first responder should jump in. Such statements as, "You know what I mean?" and "You get what I'm sayin'?" may be used to encourage a listener to join in. After an appropriate interjection from a listener, the story continues until the next opportune place for audience participation. Often there is no clear ending to the story. Sometimes a listener may take the story in a completely different direction, and sometimes the person telling the story just stops it. The story itself will tend not to move chronologically. The past may be in the middle, the present at the end, and the beginning was "another story I had to tell you before I could get to this one."

Case Study: An Account from a Memphis Firefighter

My fire company responded to a structure fire in a poverty-stricken area of town, and after extinguishing the fire, as the incident commander, I began a preliminary investigation into the cause of the fire. The resident of the home was not on the scene, but an overzealous neighbor was more than glad to give me her analysis of the situation.

Company officer: Can you tell me what happened?

Neighbor: Okay, I'm going to tell you the truth! You see, this is retaliation, you know what I'm sayin'? What had happened was last week lil' man had beat down one of the GDs, and this is retaliation. See, last week, right down the street, they all got to fightin', and lil' man got taken to 201 by the five-O, know what I'm sayin'? But now he's back out, and this is retaliation, know what I'm sayin'? So today this hoopty comes rolling by and throws some of those cocktails through that window right there and started that fire, know what I'm sayin'? This is retaliation, know what I'm sayin'?

Company officer: I have no idea what you are saying! Do you know who it was?

Neighbor: Oh, no.

Company officer: Can you describe the vehicle or the individuals?

Neighbor: Oh! No! I can't do that, you know what I'm sayin'?

Case Study: Walter

The following story from *Bridges Out of Poverty* is based on an actual court case heard in Houston, Texas, during March 1995.[16] The **bold** print indicates the "narrator's" story that came out in the trial; the plain print indicates the kinds of comments that might be made by others if this were a story being told in generational poverty by a relative or neighbor.

Well, you know Walter got put away for 37 years. Him being 48 and all. He'll probably die in jail. Just couldn't leave his hands off that 12-year-old Susie.

Dirty old man. Bodding's gonna whup his tail.

Already did. You know Bodding was waiting for him in jail and beat the living daylights out of him.

In jail?

Yeah, Bodding got caught for possession. Had $12,000 on him when they arrested him.

Golly, wish I had been there to cash in! (laughter) A man's gotta make a living!

Susie being blind and all—I can see why Bodding beat the daylights out of Walter. Lucky he didn't get killed, old Walter is.

Too bad her momma is no good.

She started the whole thing! Susie's momma goes over there and argues with Bodding.

Ain't they divorced?

Yeah, and she's got Walter working for her, repairing her house or something.

Or something, I bet. What's she got in her house that's worth fixing?

Anyway, she goes over to Bodding's house to take the lawn-mower...

I reckon so as Walter can mow the yard? I bet that's the first time old Walter has ever broken a sweat! Reminds me of the time I saw Walter thinking about taking a job. All that thinking, and he had to get drunk. He went to jail that time, too—a felony, I think it was. So many of those DWIs. Judge told him he was egregious. Walter said he wasn't greasy—he took a bath last week! (laughter)

Bodding and Susie's momma got in a fight, so she tells Walter to take Susie with him.

Lordy, her elevator must not go all the way to the top! Didn't she know about him getting arrested for enticing a minor?

With Susie blind and all. And she sends Susie with Walter?

She sure don't care about her babies.

Well, Walter's momma was there 'cause Walter lives with his momma, seeing as how he can't keep no job.

Ain't his other brother there?

Yeah, and him 41 years old. That poor momma sure has her burdens to bear. And then her 30-year-old daughter, Susie's

momma, at home too. You know Susie's momma lost custody of her kids. Walter gets these videos, you know. Those adult videos. Heavy breathing! (laughter)

Some of them are more fun to listen to than look at! (laughter) Those people in the videos are des-per-ate!

Anyway, he puts those on and then carries Susie to his room and tells her she wants him—and describes all his sex-u-al exploits!

Golly, he must be a loooooooooover. (laughter) He should be shot. I'd kill him if he did that to my kid!

Then he lets his fingers do the walking.

Kinda like the Yellow Pages! (laughter)

I guess he didn't do anything with his "thang," according to Miss Rosie who went to that trial every day. And Susie begging him to stop so many times.

Probably couldn't do anything with it; that's why he needs to listen to that heavy breathing! Pant! Pant! (laughter) What a no-count, low-down creep. I'll pay Bodding to kill him!

Bodding says the only way Walter is coming out of jail is in a pine box.

Don't blame him myself.

Yeah, Miss Rosie said Walter's momma said at the trial that the door to Walter's room was open, and there ain't no way Walter could have done that. That she is a good Christian momma and she don't put up with that.

Oh Lordy, did God strike her dead on the spot, or is she still alive? I'd be afraid of ending up in eternal damnation for telling a story like that!

Miss Rosie said her 12-year-old nephew testified that the door was closed and his grandma told him to say it was open!

Ooo! Ooo! Oooo! That poor baby tells the truth? His grandma's gonna make him mis-er-a-ble!

And then Walter's momma tells that jury that she never allows those adult videos in her house, leastways not that she pays for them! (lots of laughter)

I bet the judge bit on that one! How is Walter gonna get videos except for her money? Mowing yards? (more laughter) No, I bet he saves his pennies! (laughter)

All these years she has covered for Walter. Guess she just couldn't cover no more.

Remember that time Walter got drunk and wrecked her car, and she said she was driving? And she was at the hospital at the time with a broken leg. And the judge asked her how she could be driving and in the hospital "simultaneously." And she said that's just how it was—simultaneously—she had never felt so excited in her life. (laughter) Who turned Walter in?

Well, it wasn't Susie's momma. She was busy with Skeeter, her new boyfriend. I hear he's something.

Remember that one boyfriend she had? Thought he was so smart?

Speaking of smart, that Susie sure is. Her blind and all, and she won the district spelling bee for the seventh grade this year. I hear she's in National Honor Society, whatever that is.

Wonder if it's kinda like the country club. Instead of playing golf, you just spell! (laughter)

Susie calls this friend of hers who tells her mother and they come and get her and take her to the police and hospital.

Some rich lady, not minding her own business, that's for sure.

Well, it was a good thing for Susie, 'cause that momma of hers sure ain't good for Susie. She don't deserve a kid like Susie. *She* oughta be the one who's blind.

Ain't that the truth. Way I see it, she already is. Just look at Skeeter! (gales of laughter)

If first responders hear a story like this and get frustrated, their nonverbals will communicate that frustration—unless they have learned to control them. If you work in law enforcement and give off even just a few negative nonverbals, your witness will either shut down on you or confront you. In the case that the witness confronts you, the scenario often plays out something like this: The witness says, "So you think you're mister big guy just 'cause you got a badge and a gun? I don't need this crap! I got things at home I need to take care of," and starts to walk away. You call the witness back, but also recall the hidden rules: Because there is no relationship in place, this witness may not come back. This lack of feeling beholden to cooperate may be expressed verbally, as in, "You don't mean nothin' to me!" So the person keeps walking. If your next move is to immobilize the person on the hood of your squad car and make an arrest for either obstructing the investigation or fleeing, you may find that the person is still "mouthing off" to you as you make the arrest. "Oh, you think you're real big now just 'cause you got a badge, a gun, and handcuffs. Yeah, you're a real big man now. Just for the record, I've had the handcuffs on tighter!"

When people in this situation get to jail, they feel they have been completely and totally wronged. In addition, law enforcement personnel feel more frustration with the population than ever before—all because of a huge but generally unrecognized miscommunication.

TOOL

When you encounter a circular story spoken in casual register, do three things:

First, listen to the story to gather a clear idea of the information. Enjoy the story—it is meant to be entertaining, and it usually is. If you are a police officer, note that many times the story will also include useful information for you regarding other things in the neighborhood. Though I may be answering your questions about the description of the person who robbed the corner store, I might also say, "Well, Jackie—y'know, the girl selling outta her car over on 42nd—well, she's been seeing the guy who robbed the store, and I don't like her at all." Did you need to know that I don't like Jackie? No, but knowing that she's dating the suspect may be useful later. Numerous small pieces

(continued on next page)

(continued from previous page)

TOOL

of information flow out of a story when witnesses feel comfortable talking. Listen for those pieces of information. Let things you don't need to hear about roll past you; however, if a potentially important point is unclear, jump in: "Your old man's cousin? Now, how does he fit into all of this again?"

Sometimes you will not have time to hear a long, circular story. In these cases you may need to interrupt someone, but the interruption will be better received if you say something like this: "This sounds like a great story, and I appreciate you telling me, but in order for me to help your community (or your friend), I'm gonna need to cut you off and ask you exactly what he looks like. Once I have that description and I can get the rest of the department looking for this guy, then I can listen to the rest of the story. Okay? So, tell me exactly what color cap did he have on?" The point here is to honor the fact that someone is talking to you, state that you're interrupting in order to help the community or someone with whom the person has a relationship, and show that you will let the person tell the story in the future. Be sure to return and listen to the story so that you can collect those small pieces of information discussed above.

Second, always watch your nonverbals. If you need information for an arrest, you need to be conscious of the message your nonverbals are sending. Negative nonverbals will lead to a witness shutting down or confronting you. Either response makes law enforcement personnel less successful at retrieving useful information.

Finally, after the witness is done telling you the information, tell it back to the witness in formal register as a way to clarify. Take it slow. If it was hard for you to understand the story in casual register, it is equally hard for some people to follow the story in formal register. However, retelling the story in formal register ensures that you've collected accurate information.

Future Orientation, Choice, and Power

If an individual depends upon a random, episodic story structure for memory patterns, lives in an unpredictable environment, and has not developed the ability to plan, then...

If individuals cannot plan, they cannot predict.

If individuals cannot predict, they cannot identify cause and effect.

If individuals cannot identify cause and effect, they cannot identify consequence.

If individuals cannot identify consequence, they cannot control impulsivity.

If individuals cannot control impulsivity, they have an inclination toward criminal behavior.

Adapted from the work of Reuven Feuerstein

Source: *Bridges Out of Poverty*[17]

When no one intervenes, law enforcement personnel in particular see the scenario described above play out in a short period of time. Let's examine it point by point.

If an individual depends upon a random, episodic story structure for memory patterns... The story structure with which we're most comfortable also affects our patterns of memory. An individual whose memories are primarily stored according to the casual register story structure retains information in a sporadic, circular manner. But most first responders ask for information in a linear, chronological form. This has an impact on a department's effectiveness in interviewing.

...lives in an unpredictable environment... The mental model of poverty demonstrates that many citizens from poverty do not have the privilege of living in a stable environment.

…does not have the ability to plan… Police officers often witness this element. I frequently hear officers say things like, "Jodi, he knew step one, but two and three seemed to elude him."

…cannot predict… This means that the person is not taking the information or moment at hand and thinking about how it will play out in the future. This occurs when one is concerned about surviving and is less invested in a future scenario.

…cannot identify consequence… Think about the witness from poverty who walked away from a police officer even as the officer told her to come back. That woman probably wasn't thinking, "Oh, wait a minute, if I don't listen to the officer, then he can arrest me, which means I spend at least two days in jail until I am arraigned and out. That would be two days everyone would be at my apartment without me, and I am supposed to work tomorrow." If one does not process each step above, then you can begin to see how that person may not see consequences coming.

Police officers and other first responders have seen this process played out by citizens they work with. The following scenario plays out daily across the nation in all aspects of emergency response. You are called to a domestic disturbance with injury at 2 a.m., requiring both police and medical emergency response. This location is one where calls for emergency response services, particularly police, are frequent. It is a warm night in the middle of the week. The door is open when you arrive.

As you enter, you see several children up and running about. Tomorrow is a school day, and they will be expected to attend school in the morning, just a few hours from now. Multiple dogs and cats are all over the property and in and out of the house. There is no food in the house, and the television is on. What is the volume of the television? *Loud.* Always loud, as it is entertainment (an important component in poverty), and in order to be heard and enjoyed, it must overcome all other noise. There is hostility evident between the adult parties involved in the domestic disturbance. Children are crying, and both adults are yelling at each other. Everyone is trying to talk at the same time, the kids are crying, the television is blaring, the dogs are barking.

Imagine the impact on children growing up in this environment using the information from Feuerstein documented above. What are the long-term consequences?

The next morning, the 13-year-old from this home is walking to school, several blocks away, and he passes by a convenience store. Cutting across the parking lot, he notices an unlocked car with its engine running. Without hesitation, the young boy jumps behind the wheel of the car and drives away. Where does he go with his newfound transportation? Why, to school, of course! At school, where everyone knows he is neither old enough to drive nor the owner of a car, he is subsequently arrested.

When confronted by police, the question asked of our larceny suspect is, "Why did you steal this car and drive it to school? You had to know you would be caught and arrested once you got to school."

His answer is a simple "I don't know," and his driving to school makes it clear that when he stole the car, he had no immediate knowledge of the consequences. The old adage "it seemed like a good idea at the time" is the best answer to why he took the car when clearly he did not leave home that morning with auto theft on his mind. Living in a chaotic environment where he cannot plan, predict, or identify consequence has resulted in exactly what Feuerstein suggests: impulsive behavior, which in this case is criminal. We often see these instances identified as "crimes of opportunity."

While it is helpful to understand the cycle, the tools below can actually prevent it from occurring.

TOOL

Utilize these three concepts
during your encounters:
future orientation, choice,
and power.

In the sequence outlined on the previous page, people may not see
the consequences coming (future orientation), may feel that there is
no choice in the matter, and/or may feel like there is no opportunity
to voice objections; consequently, people in this situation can feel
like things just happen to them (no feeling of power).

Future orientation, choice, and power are three concepts that offer
people ways to reframe their encounters with first responders and
can stop cycles like the one outlined above from occurring. If one
is processing this moment in terms of the future, one tends to see
consequences; if one feels one has power and knows the choices
available, then one can choose other actions and avoid going
through each step of the cycle outlined above. Sharing these three
concepts with the people you encounter ensures that they see what
is coming and feel they have choice and power in the situation. The
next tool is a practical way to utilize this.

TOOL

"If you choose, then you have
chosen," is a sentence that
enhances the concepts in the
last tool: future orientation,
choice, and power.

A sentence I must use 50 times a day when I'm in the field is, "If you choose X, then you've chosen Y." This simple sentence enhances all three concepts—future orientation, choice, and power. Let's break this down point by point as well.

If you... This means that the individual is in control and has power.

...choose... This teaches that there are choices.

...then... This strengthens the concept of cause and effect.

...you've chosen... This builds future orientation and awareness of consequences.

Though this sentence nurtures all three crucial concepts, it must always be used twice to illustrate at least two options. Saying only, "If you choose to keep your music up loud, then you've chosen a fine," doesn't do a sufficient job of presenting the concept of power through choice. Use the sentence structure twice. Say, "Or, if you choose to turn it down so your neighbors quit calling, you've chosen not to see me again today and to spend that $200 on something cool instead of on a public nuisance ticket." Be a fork in the road so that citizens on the verge of making harmful or costly decisions can pause and reconsider. It can be hard not to take some behaviors personally, but one has to remember that one doesn't know what a given citizen has been through that day. Some have been battered, some haven't eaten, some are unsure where they will live next week. Present a civilian with the opportunity to consider: You choose this behavior, and here is what you have chosen; you choose this other behavior, and you've chosen something entirely different.

Reframing: Making Information Meaningful by Tapping into Citizens' Motivation

It is vital that whatever you say after "then you have chosen…" be meaningful to the citizen, but please note that it doesn't necessarily have to be meaningful to you. For example, let's say you work for a police department and you have a domestic call in a middle class neighborhood involving a man who is alleged to have assaulted his wife. When you arrive on the scene, you separate everyone, ensure that the scene is safe, and start talking to the victim. As you speak to her, her husband starts to get upset. You turn to him and say, "Hey, settle down or I will have to take you to jail." This is a very meaningful statement to most middle class men because their thinking is future-oriented. The badge represents power in their community, and the instability caused by going to jail can threaten their achievement. The middle class husband sees immediately that getting arrested in front of the neighbors will not be good for his or his family's reputation, not to mention the fact that his wife will have to bail him out, a burden both financial and emotional. The future ramifications start to outweigh the current situation.

People in middle class also see information and institutions as ways to maintain some power in a situation, so the man might say, "Fine, I'll settle down. I would like your name and badge number. I will take this up with your superiors." The middle class man can maintain some power and control in the moment by gathering information he can use later to file a complaint with the department, the institution that wields power over citizens and individual first responders. The point is that the information you presented was meaningful to the recipient, and the recipient demonstrated knowledge of the three concepts by taking what you said, thinking about how it would play out in the future, seeing a choice, and finding a way to maintain power in the situation. Therefore, the statement you made to him as a first responder was ultimately effective.

Now let's imagine the same scene as it might transpire in poverty. Same domestic call, you have everyone separated, you are talking to the victim, and the man starts to get upset. If you say the same sentence in poverty that you used in middle class, "Hey, settle down or I will have to take you to jail," it tends not to have the same effect because it isn't nearly as meaningful to the person in poverty. He is focused on the right now, and your badge alone is not enough to convince him of your power and authority. It is not that this man is not motivated—he is—but the concerns that motivate him are very different than the concerns that motivate the man in middle class. Say something like this: "Hey, Fred is it? I see what you're sayin'. I patrol this area, and I've seen Bob hanging out over here. I've never seen your lady talk to him, but I see him in this area. All I am sayin' is that if you don't settle down and work with me, you know I gotta take you in. What is it, about two days in jail before they let you out and you can get back here? That's two days Bob would be running around the neighborhood free while you're locked up." Even though Fred may not want to work with law enforcement, he wants even less to leave Bob alone in the community, especially around his family and his partner. Now you have reframed your information in a way that makes it meaningful to Fred and enhances the concepts of future orientation, choice, and power. The more first responders understand the communities they serve, the more they can transfer information about laws and regulations in ways that are meaningful enough to tap into anyone's motivation; this keeps first responders safer and makes the job easier.

The problem is not that citizens are not motivated; the problem is that we often fail to make our information appeal to the factors that motivate each citizen. This is one of the main challenges facing people who choose emergency response as a career. First responders do not get to choose their clients. They must serve the poorest of the poor and wealthiest of the wealthy—and they must hold them all accountable to the same standards and laws.

Accountability

Accountability is a key concept, and I make a point to emphasize its importance in my trainings. It is almost impossible to create a relationship of mutual respect with people if you do not hold each other accountable within the relationship. It is because I love and respect my family that I am also going to be honest with them, hold them accountable to a certain standard, and expect them to do the same for me. In this way, holding people accountable can be a form of respect. Law enforcement officers have a clear standard to uphold—the law—which cannot be lowered. Still, if law enforcement officers try to meet that standard by using the hidden rules from their own communities, rather than the hidden rules of the community they are working in, those officers will find themselves stressed out and increasingly ineffective. The same will happen if officers assume that people have resources they do not, or if they communicate using only one register and one story structure. Those officers also run the risk of seeming hypocritical if they are acting in this manner and at the same time demanding accountability. Accountability keeps our society safe and so must be demanded from every citizen. But the way in which that accountability is demanded is a key determinant of one's justness and fairness. The more tools first responders have that work for each particular community, the more meaningful they'll be able to make the information, the better they can stay in control, and the safer and easier their jobs will be.

Voices

Most people have all three voices and have used them before. The child voice is the one we turn to when we want to "whine" about the supervisor, as in, "The supervisor likes you more than me! You got your vacation request approved and I didn't!"

The parent voice is the one we turn to when we want to take control. If a fire broke out, I would use my parent voice to take control. "You, get out over there! You, go to the right!"

In contrast, if I were teaching a group of people how to evacuate a room in case of a fire, I would use the adult voice. Teaching occurs in the adult voice. When first responders need to take control of a situation, they will often use the parent voice. However, in the last three minutes on a call, when they are trying to say something that will prevent them from having to come back, they will want to use the adult voice, which is the best voice for fostering learning. If they use the parent voice to try to teach the concepts when there is no immediate threat, people may feel that they are being patronized and/or bossed around and will not respond well.

Three Voices

Adapted from the work of Eric Berne

The Child Voice

Defensive, victimized, emotional, whining, losing attitude, strongly negative nonverbal

☐ Quit picking on me.

☐ You don't love me.

☐ You want me to leave.

☐ Nobody likes (loves) me.

☐ I hate you.

☐ You're ugly.

☐ You make me sick.

☐ It's your fault.

☐ Don't blame me.

☐ She, he, _____ did it.

☐ You make me mad.

☐ You made me do it.

The child voice is also playful, spontaneous, curious, etc.
The phrases listed often occur in conflictual or manipulative situations and impede resolution.

The Parent Voice

Authoritative, directive, judgmental, evaluative, win-lose mentality, demanding, punitive, sometimes threatening

- ☐ You shouldn't (should) do that.
- ☐ It's wrong (right) to do _____ .
- ☐ That's stupid, immature, out of line, ridiculous.
- ☐ Life's not fair. Get busy.
- ☐ You are good, bad, worthless, beautiful (any judgmental, evaluative comment).

- ☐ You do as I say.
- ☐ If you weren't so _____ , this wouldn't happen to you.
- ☐ Why can't you be like _____ ?

The parent voice also can be very loving and supportive. The phrases listed usually occur during conflict and impede resolution. The internal parent voice can create shame and guilt.

The Adult Voice

Not judgmental, free of negative nonverbals, factual, often in question format, attitude of win-win

- ☐ In what ways could this be resolved?
- ☐ What factors will be used to determine the effectiveness, quality of _____ ?
- ☐ I would like to recommend _____ .
- ☐ What are choices in this situation?
- ☐ I am comfortable (uncomfortable) with _____ .
- ☐ Options that could be considered are _____ .
- ☐ For me to be comfortable, I need the following things to occur _____ .
- ☐ These are the consequences of that choice/action _____ .
- ☐ We agree to disagree.

Source: *Bridges Out of Poverty*[18]

TOOL

Many children in poverty possess and use the parent voice.

Due to the instability that is caused by trying to survive in poverty, some older children must care for their younger siblings. Thus, some children learn to use the parent voice out of necessity. Children in this situation are very likely to respond negatively if a first responder with whom they don't have a relationship speaks to them in the parent voice. In the child's view, the child is the one who uses that voice (the parent voice)—not the first responders. Couple this with the fact that the child is more invested in this moment than in the future and it becomes easy to understand why the child gets upset with the first responders.

Children in middle class, on the other hand, often respond to the parent voice by backing off. This is because power in middle class is often associated with position and because there is an emphasis on future stories and ramifications. The child associates the uniform and the badge with a position of power, hears a voice of authority from that person of power, sees the ramifications of noncompliance, and generally complies. The tools within this book are meant to be used after a scene or situation is under control; therefore, all the tools should be conducted in the adult voice.

Conclusion

The register of language to which people were exposed most while growing up affects their communication patterns. First responders quickly learn that not all citizens communicate in the same register or with the same story structure. While some communities emphasize nonverbal communication, other communities rely heavily on verbal communication. While some will use words for negotiation, others will use words of survival. Likewise, the three voices every person has—parent, child, and adult—will get different responses in different situations and communities. For example, as law enforcement personnel master the information in the language section and understand how it affects the people they serve and protect, they will find that getting information from witnesses becomes easier, their questioning of suspects becomes more powerful, and they are better able to hold people accountable. The bottom line is that law enforcement personnel can make tactical use of this information regarding communication just as they would be tactical in monitoring a protest or raiding a known drug house.

When we understand the nature of the three voices (child, parent, and adult), we can see that first responders use the parent voice to gain control in chaotic situations. We must also understand and acknowledge that the parent voice may be overused in situations where an adult voice of reason and cooperation would be a better fit. Looking for opportunities to use the adult voice and not taking offense when adults use the child voice are methods of tactical communication that may help de-escalate situations.

When utilized to its fullest, tactical communication will increase a first responder's effectiveness and safety within all three economic communities.

Chapter Four
Resources

Crisis = When an individual has few or no resources to draw upon in a given situation.

The table on the following page lists the eight resources originally identified by Ruby Payne in *A Framework for Understanding Poverty*.[19] It also includes three additional resources identified by Philip DeVol in collaboration with people from poverty during the development of *Getting Ahead in a Just-Gettin'-By World*. The table reproduced here is from *Getting Ahead*.

Definition of Resources

Resource	Definition
Financial	Having the money to purchase goods and services.
Emotional	Being able to choose and control emotional responses, particularly to negative situations, without engaging in self-destructive behavior. This is an internal resource and shows itself through stamina, perseverance, and choices.
Mental	Having the mental abilities and acquired skills (reading, writing, computing) to deal with daily life.
Spiritual	Believing in divine purpose and guidance.
Physical	Having physical health and mobility.
Support systems	Having friends, family, and backup resources available to access in times of need. These are external resources.
Relationships/ role models	Having frequent access to adult(s) who are appropriate, who are nurturing to the child, and who do not engage in self-destructive behavior.
Knowledge of hidden rules	Knowing the unspoken cues and habits of a group.
Integrity and trust	Trust is linked to two issues: predictability and safety. Can I know with some certainty that this person will do what they say? Can I predict with some accuracy that it will occur every time? The second part of the question is safety: Will I be safe with this person?
Motivation and persistence	Having the energy and drive to prepare for, plan, and complete projects, jobs, and personal changes.
Formal register	Having the vocabulary, language ability, and negotiation skills to succeed in work and/or school environments.

Source: *Getting Ahead in a Just-Gettin'-By World* [20]

More Than Just Money

Resources affect the stability individuals, institutions, and communities will be able to demonstrate and maintain. In the United States we have often looked at poverty as a one-resource issue, by which I mean we examine the financial aspect of poverty and call the case closed. However, there are many resources in play. In fact, the graphic on the previous page identifies 11 resources that are directly related to the issue. Please note that people in poverty analyzed this information and contributed the last three resources because they felt these were so essential they needed to be included.

First responders have spoken about coming into contact with citizens who have an abundance of financial resources (a person could have $20 million to her name), but because their other 10 resources are underdeveloped, they have a difficult time maintaining stable circles. On the other hand, first responders have met families who are struggling economically, yet they are rich in the other 10 resources. Those families often are able to maintain a higher level of stability in their circles and lives than are others in their neighborhoods. Due to their high level of resources, they have something to draw upon when they encounter a stressful situation. Having resources prevents the situation from escalating into a crisis. This means emergency services, especially police, usually are not called. First responders generally find themselves being called during times of crisis when resources are exhausted or unavailable. The more resources people and communities can demonstrate, the less frequently emergency intervention is needed.

Arriving at a house in middle class, the EMTs and paramedics were met by an apologetic wife. Her husband suffered from paraplegia due to a tragic hunting accident. She stated that they made arrangements with the accessible van, but it didn't come (she called them and found out it broke down and would not be fixed for several hours), and they could not afford to miss the doctor's appointment. The woman had called her children, but everyone was at work, and her husband needed his medication, but the doctor wouldn't give him a refill without seeing him. She apologized and said that really they just needed transport to the hospital. This family had resources, but when they were not accessible, they had a crisis and needed first responders' help. Many on the scene seemed sympathetic toward the couple.

Later that week there was a call to a poverty area where a man who suffered from paraplegia due to a tragic gunshot wound lived on the second floor. As he was being carried down, first responders encouraged him to get a room on the first floor. He said he put in for one when his injury happened and was on the waiting list, but it had been six months. He also stated that he had no other way to make it to his doctor's appointments, and indeed, first responders were called to his house several times more over the next year to transport him. Some first responders noted that when he was treated respectfully (verbally and nonverbally), he was very thankful. But if he saw someone roll their eyes or in some other way show their frustration with his frequent flyer status, he quickly became upset and sometimes disrespectful. When you have access to resources and only occasionally "run low," your response to—and attitude toward—the crisis may be much different than when you live in constant crisis.

TOOL

Know which resources are available in a community and which institutions help people build resources. Connect the civilian with the proper institution. The more resources people have access to, the more stability they are able to maintain, which results in fewer calls to first responders to resolve issues.

First responders will want to become aware of the resources an individual has and the resources available in the community. Knowing which resources are available and how to access them can be very beneficial on the job. While first responders do not have time to be social workers, they can often see that an individual could use assistance with a resource and can connect that individual with the person or agency that can help. If an individual does not get access to those who can assist with building a resource, this may result in further instability in that person's circle. This then increases the chances that first responders will be called upon again to deal with the same individual.

Take for example a police officer who keeps getting calls to an apartment in Section 8 housing. The mother and daughter in the apartment are always fighting. As the officer drives up to the apartment building for yet another call, he can hear the two yelling at each other from the parking lot. After separating the mother and daughter, he asks them what is going on and explains that he has been there too many times for this to be a misunderstanding. The mother states that her daughter was not listening and was not acting like herself. The officer knows of a mental health counseling service in the community, so he has the mother place a call and set up an appointment for her and her daughter. The next time he sees them in the neighborhood, he asks them how they are doing. Both report that they are doing much better and have not had law enforcement come to the apartment since they saw him last.

This story serves as an example of a first responder making an appropriate and useful recommendation because he is aware of the resources available in the community in which he works. He has also reduced the likelihood that more valuable law enforcement time will be spent resolving the issue. More importantly, he has left these citizens with a favorable view of emergency service personnel; this viewpoint will benefit all other first responders who may interact with these citizens in the future.

It is worth noting that even when people have access to resources, they may not accept them for various reasons: pride, relationships, or repercussions, perhaps. For example, when first responders arrived on a scene where a woman complained of abdominal pain, the woman said, "I am having cramps, and my water broke, and I'm about to have this baby." When asked, she did not know her due date, and she did not know how far along she was or when her last cycle was.

She had two other children, so she had obviously been through this process before. But when the first responder asked if she had seen a doctor at all during this pregnancy, she said no. The first responder knew he was going a little too far, but out of disbelief he asked the woman why she hadn't used her government assistance (it had already been established that she was receiving government assistance) to cover the cost of visits to the doctor. The woman responded, "They want to know the baby daddy's Social Security number, and he is with my friend across the street now. And she watches my babies when I am at work, and I don't want to make them mad at me for tellin', you know?"

Talking with People About Their Resources

When talking to individuals about their resources, it's best not to address deficits directly. No one responds well to this: "Hey, you're fat. Your physical resources are low. That's dangerous for your health. You need to lose weight." Rarely will this kind of "help" motivate a person to develop a resource or change a behavior. A better strategy is to address a resource that the person has a lot of before you contrast it with areas where resources are low.

A team of nurses working in a neighborhood in poverty was very frustrated that no one in the neighborhood would work to control a disease that was affecting many of them—diabetes. The nurses kept telling the adults from the community that if they did not take medicine and make appropriate lifestyle changes, they would die.

But when you live in poverty and your world is about the here and now, there are other more pressing things that could kill you sooner.

What the nurses were saying was true; however, the way in which they were presenting the information to their clients was not having the desired effect. When asked what resources their customers had a lot of, the nurses responded by saying that their relationships were very strong. With this in mind, they tried a new tack. Rather than telling their customers they were in danger of dying, the nurses asked them who would care for their grandchildren if they were not around, since many of the people at risk were raising their absent children's children. Showing them the importance of being there for their grandchildren was enough to motivate the customers to take their insulin and reevaluate their choices regarding diet, exercise, etc.

Communities and individuals are influenced by the resources available to them. When one grows up in a family or community where there is no access to jobs that pay a livable wage, reliable transportation, or relationships that nurture emotional resources and a sense of integrity, it will affect one's experience and, hence, one's behavior. When we view people in terms of the resources that they hold and the resources available in their communities, we will begin to understand how and why behaviors and experiences are different. For example, after coming off the third call in a year to a very wealthy house, a police officer stated, "I just don't get how someone with that much money can act this way and always be in crisis."

If we view stability as only being affected by one resource, money, then it's true that the behavior demonstrated is baffling. However, when we view the situation in terms of all the resources (especially emotional resources and integrity), we note that the people on the scene are visibly low in many areas; now we can begin to understand the resulting behavior. As stated earlier, understanding does not mean a first responder lowers the expectations for people, but the ability to understand the behaviors being presented makes the behaviors easier to work with and prevent in the future.

TOOL

Use a resource the civilian has a lot of in order to address resources that are not present. Many times in emergency response, the truth may be on the first responder's side, but that doesn't make the truth effective unless the first responder can enable citizens to view it in a way that makes it meaningful.

Use a resource the civilian has a lot of in order to address resources that are not present. Many times in emergency response, the truth may be on the first responder's side, but that doesn't make the truth effective unless the first responder can enable citizens to view it in a way that makes it meaningful.

When first responders see the people they serve in terms of the resources they possess, then the first responders can better understand why people are responding in one manner or another. This understanding can make the job easier and thereby reduce job-related stress, provide first responders with more choice in their responses, and ultimately keep them safer.

If first responders view all individuals and communities in terms of the resources to which they themselves have access, rather than the ones that are actually available, it will be frustrating because they will not see the behavior they expect to see. This can cause first responders a lot of stress, and in some cases it leads them to make reactionary judgments that cause loss of control of a situation—a very dangerous place to be.

Conclusion

The amount of resources one has access to and can demonstrate directly affects the stability of that person's circle (or life). When people have limited resources to draw upon, this puts them in the position of being repeatedly in crisis. First responders are called when there is a crisis. To reduce the frequency of crisis calls, one should address the resource issue.

Identify which resources civilians have a lot of, and use those resources to make your information "click" with them—to make it meaningful to them. The more meaningful it is to them, the better the chance they have of increasing their resources. Every community will look different based on the resources present. First responders can benefit greatly by knowing the resources available within the particular communities in which they work. Emergency service personnel are not social service workers, nor should they be, but the ability to link citizens with the agencies that can help them build resources (and thereby enhance the stability of their circles) can prevent first responders from being called back repeatedly to assist the same people.

It also helps a great deal for first responders to be aware of the resources they personally grew up with and to keep in mind that not all the citizens with whom they come in contact will have had the same access to resources. The goal should be to observe the resources citizens demonstrate, connect them to resources within the community when possible, make your information more meaningful by highlighting the resources civilians are rich in, understand where they are coming from without condoning unacceptable or illegal behavior, and thereby serve and protect as effectively as possible.

First responders can continue to be heroes day in and day out, but if resources continue to decline in a community, the job will be more difficult and busier than ever. In order to see a sustained, dramatic reduction in crime and other crises, resources in the community and within individuals have to be increased. If social services, educators, politicians, and community members (to name a few) do not work toward effectively building the resources in a community, first responders will continue to face a difficult job.

Chapter Five
Using This Information Throughout Your Career

In an appendix to *Bridges Out of Poverty: Strategies for Professionals and Communities* titled "Additive Model: aha! Process's Approach to Building Sustainable Communities," Phil DeVol outlines four areas of research on the causes of poverty that exist on a continuum ranging from the micro—individual choices and behaviors—to the macro—political and economic structures.[21] These areas of research and their impact and assumptions were later discussed in more detail in the workbook designed to accompany Bridges Out of Poverty workshops.[22] As you advance in your career in emergency response, the job will demand that you broaden your focus from the micro to the macro and begin to address systemic issues that allow or even perpetuate the kinds of situations first responders are called to deal with every day. Let's look now at the poverty research continuum:

Poverty Research Continuum

Causes	Behaviors of the Individual	Absence of Human and Social Capital
Research topics	Dependence on welfare	Lack of employment
	Behavior of individuals	Lack of education
	Individual morality	Inadequate skill sets
	Behaviors of groups	Decline in neighborhoods
	Single parenthood	Big government
	Intergenerational character traits	Decline in social morality
		Urbanization
	Poor parenting by mothers or fathers	Suburbanization of manufacturing
	Values held by poor, lack of work ethic, commitment	Middle class flight
		Inelastic cities, inadequate regional planning
	Breakup of families	Immigration
	Addiction, mental illness, domestic violence	Failure of social services
		Absence of knowledge, worker skills, intellectual capital
		Social capital
		Lack of career ladder between knowledge and service sectors
		Speed of economic transformation at local level

Human Exploitation	Political/Economic Structures
Minimum wage versus living wage	Policies that result in economic and social disparity
Temporary jobs	
Less than 30 hours/week	Undue influence of corporations on legislation
Lack of benefits	
Disposable employees	Tax structure that shifted tax burden to middle class, away from wealthy and corporations
Debt bondage	
Global outsourcing	Decline in wages for bottom 90%
Payday lenders	Decline of unions
Lease/purchase	Deindustrialization
Redlining	Management/labor "bargain"
Drug trade	CEO-to-line-worker salary ratio
Exploitation for markets	Profit/financial-centered form of globalization
Exploitation of resources and raw materials	
The intersection of classism and other "-isms": sexism, racism, heterosexism, ageism	

(continued on next page)

Poverty Research Continuum (continued from previous page)

Causes	Behaviors of the Individual	Absence of Human and Social Capital
Assumptions	By studying the poor, we will learn what changes individuals must make in order to climb out of poverty. The poor are somehow lacking, either because of their own bad choices or because of circumstances. They should become "like us." Poverty is a sustainable condition.	By studying human and social capital, we will learn how to work within the larger political/ economic structure to create conditions that foster prosperity. Faith that the market and market corrections will create most of the conditions necessary for general prosperity. Acceptance of a 4–5% unemployment rate as a normal feature of the economy.
What's said	Don't blame the system; change the individual. Don't upset the system.	Don't blame the political/ economic system; change the individual and the community system.

Human Exploitation	Political/Economic Structures
By studying colonial and imperialist behavior, we can learn how to create just and equitable economic structures. Dominant groups discount the legitimacy of this category and look to the future. Marginalized people (Appalachian, Black, Indigenous, people of color, former colonies) remember the past and may seek redress.	Studying the poor is not the same thing as studying poverty. Race, class, and gender are categories for analysis, not just demographics.
Upset the system and make it fair.	Don't blame the individual. Change the political/economic structure; fight poverty instead of reforming welfare.

(continued on next page)

Poverty Research Continuum (continued from previous page)

Causes	Behaviors of the Individual	Absence of Human and Social Capital
Strategies	Hold individuals accountable and use sanctions if necessary	Hold individuals and social service systems accountable
	Target individuals	Use sanctions if necessary
	Work First programs	Full employment, growth in labor market
	Self-sufficiency	Education
	Enhance language experience	Skill development
	Psychology of mind	Anti-poverty programs for childcare, child support, healthcare, and housing
	Treatment interventions	
	Resiliency	EITC (Earned Income Tax Credit)
	Work ethic	Regional planning
	Mentors	Community action programs
	Literacy	Head Start
	Asset development	Workforce Innovation and Opportunity Act
	Marriage promotion	
	Caseload reductions	Continuous growth
	All strategies focus on the individual	One-stop centers

Adapted from *Getting Ahead in a Just-Gettin'-By World* [23]

Human Exploitation	Political/Economic Structures
Hold the exploiters accountable	Hold political/economic power structure accountable
Educate all people about the power differentials within the community	Use economic disparity trends as a measure
Create an action plan to address the exploitation	Interdisciplinary approach to macroeconomic planning and policies
Community-based development	Whole-system planning
Political organizing to win control over economic and political institutions	Enhance living standards
	Redistribution of wealth in other direction
	Access to capital and ownership

Understanding these four areas of research on poverty will be a great asset to you as you advance in your career in emergency response.

When you first begin your work in emergency response, most of your time is spent dealing directly with people. The previous chapters were intended to share understanding and tools you can use when working directly with people from different economic communities. As you become a senior first responder and/or get promoted, the department will often require that your focus shift from individual interactions to a more systemic viewpoint, and you will be required to work effectively within the system. The systems that allow people in poverty you have worked with to continue to be in poverty will now be some of the main things you and your staff will have to address. The department will call on you to work not only directly with individuals but with other organizations within the community and with the community at large—maybe even at the policy level.

Receiving promotions or becoming a senior first responder generally means that you will be called to do more work with entire communities and outside agencies. In order to be effective, it will be helpful if you can identify within the four major causes of poverty the one that interests you the most and then identify the primary areas of interest of those with whom you are called to work. This will allow you to engage people where they are rather than reacting judgmentally to views that are different from your own.

Poverty has always been with us. Researchers have worked hard to try to identify the causes of poverty, not only because serving the poor takes resources, but because too much poverty can actually affect a community's and a country's stability. Therefore, if we understand all the causes of poverty, we will be able to create a holistic solution, one that doesn't simply focus on one cause but initially addresses all of the causes.

Behaviors of the Individual

The first area of research on poverty is focused on studying the behaviors of the individual in poverty. We study "Fred" in poverty. We look at Fred and his behaviors and conclude that they are the reason (or are the main contributors to) why Fred is in poverty. We research such topics as single parenthood, substance abuse, work ethic, and anything else that has to do with the individual's choices and attitude. We say things like, "This person drinks too much, and that's why he is in poverty. Too many people are single parents; that's why there is poverty. Fred in poverty has a poor work ethic; that's the cause of poverty."

One of the assumptions underlying this area of research is that by studying the poor we will learn what new behaviors individuals will have to learn so they can pull themselves out of poverty. Strategies or solutions that are a direct result of this area of research are programs like Work First. Surely if Fred gets a job, then he will be out of poverty; therefore, create a Work First program, and never mind that the job Fred obtains does not pay a livable wage—that is not the focus. Fred is working—that is the point. The research focused on Fred, so the solution will depend on Fred. Do you see solutions in the communities in which you work that are strictly based on the individual? There is a good chance that they are products of the research done regarding the behaviors of the individual.

Human and Social Capital in the Community

The second area of research on poverty is human and social capital within the community. Here there is a focus on factors within the community that cause poverty. That Fred is in poverty is not just due to Fred; the community in which Fred lives is the main contributing factor that keeps him in poverty. Research will show that poverty communities often have less livable wage jobs, test scores are often lower in schools, zoning laws are different, and funding is not the same. Therefore, the solutions are community-based. Get local businesses to pay a livable wage, and we will end poverty. Make the school system produce stronger results, and we will end poverty.

Robert Putnam writes in his book *Bowling Alone* about human and social capital declining in many neighborhoods in the United States—not just in poverty—meaning we don't know our neighbors and are therefore less likely to assist each other.[24] Community groups, lodges, clubs, and leagues are declining in membership. One role these organizations played was to ensure that communities knew each other and cared for each other. From a community not providing livable wage jobs to the decline in social capital that Putnam writes about, this area of research focuses on the community and how factors therein contribute to the causes of poverty.

Human Exploitation

The third area of research focuses on exploitation of people and communities. This area of research concludes that as long as individuals and communities are treated differently based on economic background, gender, race, age, and/or sexual orientation, then there will continue to be poverty. The fact that classism (the belief that because you come from a certain class you have different abilities) exists is one of the main causes of poverty. This area of research will often focus on naming the exploitation and solving the problem by raising awareness of the exploitation, examining how the exploitation affects everyone (not just those being exploited), and calling for a particular action. Robert Jensen's book *The Heart of Whiteness* is a great example of someone clearly naming an exploitation, analyzing how it has affected him and the group of people he represents, and calling for action.[25] Exploitation can be very complicated as it can occur in many ways to numerous people. For example, one person might experience the "benefits" of being part of the dominant gender group while simultaneously being exploited due to age, race, or any other factor. Therefore, the focus of this area is not to point the finger at just one group and place blame; rather, it is to name the ways in which one group of people wields more power than another group because of its class, gender, race, age, sexual orientation, etc.; to analyze the negative effects for everyone (not just those who are being exploited); and to call all parties to a direct action.

Political and Economic Structures

The fourth and final area of research focuses on political and economic structures. This area focuses on city, county, state, and federal policies that favor one economic class over another. Researchers here will study which group of people has the most influence on legislators and the resulting policies that are passed. It researches how the tax structure is set up and points to the people/entities it benefits most. The solution here, in contrast to the solution posed by the first area of research, focuses on creating fair economic and political systems. The focus is on the system, not on the individual.

In his book *Wealth and Democracy,* Kevin Phillips analyzes the wealthy class and how policies and political influence have helped the wealthy maintain their wealth and become wealthier throughout the history of the United States.[26] Though the book examines some individuals, the focus is on how those individuals' actions influenced political and economic structures to favor the wealthy, often at the expense of the middle class and those in poverty.

Finding Your Focus and Understanding Other Views

Many people develop a "favorite" area of research, meaning one that they feel has a greater impact than the others. Most people also have a "least favorite" area of research, one they don't believe has as much legitimacy as the others. It's my guess that as you read about the four areas of research, one in particular clicked with you and made you think, "Yeah, that's it! That's what causes poverty." That area of research may well be the one you will (or already have) come to emphasize. This cause of poverty and the solutions that stem from it will be easy for you to discuss with other people. However, as you become a senior first responder, it is likely that you will be called to work with many partners, all of whom will have their own favorite areas as well. In order to be effective within these community meetings, you will need to be aware of what your favorite area of research is and be able to identify what areas of research are most interesting to others.

Within a given community, those who favor the causes that fall under the individual behavior category will often find themselves polarized against those who favor causes related to political and economic structures. One group is saying poverty is caused by the individual, and the other group is saying that poverty is caused by the system. As a high-ranking member of the emergency response community, you will be called upon to address causes that fall under all of these categories. In fact, it is imperative that any community working to reduce poverty address all four areas if it wishes to be effective.

TOOL

All four areas of research will have to be addressed if a community wants to effectively reduce poverty. Be aware of your community partners' favorite areas of research when you work with them, but don't forget to be aware of your own preference as well.

All four areas of research are legitimate. Does Fred in poverty make individual choices? You better believe he does! Does the community influence those decisions? Certainly. We have all seen a child with potential get sucked into the criminal activities of the neighborhood. Is there exploitation? Any first responder who has worked in both extremely wealthy and extremely poor neighborhoods can tell you about the different levels of access the two classes have because of their different levels of income. And we have all seen how political and economic structures have affected the neighborhoods we work with.

In his book *American Dream,* Jason DeParle shares the stories of three women from generational poverty. However, as he tells their stories, he also writes about the political and economic policies being drafted, passed, and implemented at the same time. Some of the policies meant to address poverty do not affect these women at all; some have a direct impact on them. Through the course of this book, DeParle makes it clear that every administration, whether Republican or Democratic, had its "favorite" area of research and put policies in place to address that area.[27] But, in order to address poverty successfully, we will need to deal with all four areas of research during the same time period.

This means that both of the participants who raise their hands during my presentation have legitimate arguments—one stating loudly, "Poverty is all Fred's fault! If he would just get off his butt, get a job, and do what he has to do, then we wouldn't have poverty!" and the participant in the next seat exclaiming just as loudly, "It is not Fred's fault! If there were more fair trade than free trade, we wouldn't have lost all our decent-paying factory jobs. If lobbyists funded by the rich didn't have so much influence, then we wouldn't have poverty! Political and economic structures cause it!" Both of these participants have legitimate arguments, and both will have to be listened to and addressed if we are ever going to decrease or eliminate poverty.

Knowing the area of research you relate to most is essential to working effectively within a community. Understanding what areas the other participants favor and being able to understand their viewpoints is crucial. Being able to bring everyone to the table and make them feel that their viewpoints are legitimate while honoring their neighbors' viewpoints will cause you to be viewed as an effective leader. That makes your job easier and your department's public image more favorable.

Emergency Response Leadership: Applying This Material in the Department and in Society at Large

This information can be useful for first responders throughout their careers. There are four areas in which first responders can use this information: within individual interactions, within the departments or institutions for which they work, within the communities in which they work and live, and within the area of policy-level decisions. As we discussed in earlier chapters, a first responder's career often begins with a lot of direct contact with individuals from different economic backgrounds. The previous chapters are meant to help first responders better understand the complex ways in which economic class influences people and their actions. Armed with

Source: J Pfarr Consulting

this understanding, a first responder can choose their next response, rather than just react. Reacting often means the first responder is no longer in control, and that is dangerous. Understanding what is happening in front of you allows you to choose what the next move is. This allows a first responder the opportunity to be viewed as a good leader. Being viewed as a good leader gets you respect in the community and ultimately makes the job easier.

Using this information at the individual level alone is often insufficient, especially after one has been promoted to a senior position. To gain the most from this information, an emergency service worker will want to apply it in all four areas. If we do not implement this information at the departmental, community, and policy levels, we will not change the system or the community; therefore, first responders who come after you will continue to face the same or even greater challenges. In order to have a long-term effect, this information must be used within all four areas.

Application Within Emergency Response Organizations

At times I hear first responders state that they try to take the time to build more relationships with individuals within the different communities, but the department does not support their efforts. These first responders are caught in a triangle with their departments and the individuals they serve, and most times it is the departments that dictate acceptable interactions between first responders and citizens.

Typically, emergency responders' performance is assessed by looking at the number of calls for service and the end results of those calls. For police, examination of arrests, citations issued, and warrants served, along with a look at the number of calls for service and reports created, is the most commonly used method of performance assessment. These data, while important for showing that an individual or agency is productive, are geared toward the goal of counting police activity rather than tracking criminal activity in each area, neighborhood, or community. None of the above statistics prove a reduction in crime, number of crimes solved, or an improvement in police-community relations. These statistics do not do much to make a community feel safe, nor do they enhance police-community relationships.

We know zero tolerance policing produces high numbers of arrests. However, if we are searching for another type of metric for assessing performance, we might investigate options that reinforce community policing concepts and are consistent with *Tactical Communication* recommendations for relationship building. Examples include but are not limited to:

- Tracking crime reported in a defined geographic area to identify trends, increases, or decreases. Once relationships are established and assessments for other resources are identified and brought to bear, responders can be rewarded for concepts that reduce calls for service or criminal activity in those same pre-identified geographic areas. Responder performance is assessed based on positive results.

- For law enforcement, arrests and successful prosecutions must be included in the overall strategy for crime reduction and holding criminals accountable, but high numbers of arrests that do not reduce crime or lead to successful prosecutions should not be the sole metric for judging performance.

- Identifying opportunities for developing relationships that produce information to solve crimes. The cultivation of relationships with the community should be a metric resulting in reward or commendation if those relationships lead to citizen cooperation that results in arrests, successful prosecution, and problem-solving.

- Assessing citizen satisfaction with responder performance and how citizens gauge the relationship with responders, including fire and medical. Polls conducted to ascertain public attitudes toward responders can help determine whether methods are well-received and successful or need to be changed or even abandoned.

This information must be used within the institution or department as much as it is used with individuals. Begin to think about how this information can be used during the training of new hires, during the hiring process, and in the way the department operates. For example, who created the questions for hiring? Were they generated by personnel who are from one class? If a person from wealth wrote all of the questions in the interview, would a person from wealth or middle class have an unfair (yet unnoticed) advantage when answering them? Some departments have integrated this information into the training in the academy as a way to prepare their first responders. Other departments have used the information (especially this last chapter) to prepare their first responders when moving from a focus on individual interactions to a focus on community and/or systemic issues.

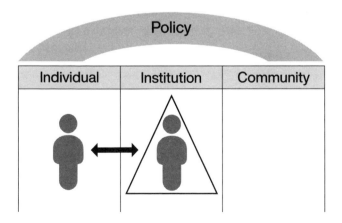

Source: J. Pfarr Consulting

Application in the Community

The events that occur within the community absolutely affect the department, as well as the first responders' individual interactions. Emergency responders can attest to the positive results of having access to sufficient livable wage jobs, banking or lending institutions, green spaces, activities for youth, and schools with adequate funding, positive and caring cultures, and low student-to-teacher ratios.

Law enforcement has, over time, seen its role within the community as a crucial one, and in many of our communities you will see officers in schools participating in after-school programs, assisting with fundraising, and doing community policing. As first responders implement this information within the community, it will become clear that policies guide and influence what is possible within the community.

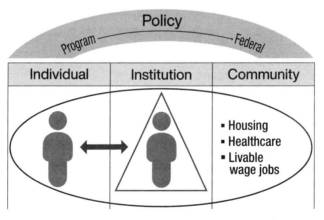

Source: J Pfarr Consulting

Application at the Policy Level

The fourth and final way to implement this information is by reviewing policies. This includes policies of the department, the city, the county, all the way up to federal policies. Policies directly and indirectly influence departments and individual interactions.

Think about the policies many states have put in place regarding pseudoephedrine and how that has affected the illegal production of methamphetamine. Begin to think about how the information in the previous chapters can be used to shape policies within the department and at the city and state levels. Again, go back to the policies that regulate hiring: Are any of them geared toward one class more than another?

Many first responders' view on policies and procedures is that "policy exists because someone screwed up." But policies and procedures are often put in place to push personnel toward proven best practices. When dealing with persons in generational poverty, consider these policies and procedures in order to build an effective community policing program using *Tactical Communication* concepts.

For law enforcement, is there a written policy on alternatives to arrest, and are the alternatives meaningful, easy to navigate, and encouraged by the agency?

In some cases, agencies initiate programs for alternatives to arrest, but the results are not successful. If officers are not "buying in" to the options, it may be because:

- The alternatives are more work for officers than simple arrests. For example, they may require more paperwork or take longer to navigate.

- Officers don't fully understand how the programs work and don't trust the results.

- Officers believe the programs are "soft on crime."

- Alternatives have been tried before and failed or lacked sustainability.

- Referrals to alternatives to arrest are not tracked or shown in performance evaluations, whereas arrests are.

Are there responders serving on the boards, councils, and committees of organizations that serve people from poverty?

In order to build relationships with not only persons in poverty but also those providing services and resources, responders should volunteer or be assigned to serve on service providers' governing groups. This must be a system in which the right person is picked, and the overall strategy must be one that gets the buy-in of the agency and its personnel. Assigning people who don't wish to serve or who will undermine, be apathetic, or refuse to attend meetings can harm the agency and the relationship-building process.

What methods and metrics are used to assess responder performance? Are the metrics used consistent with a community-oriented approach, such as identified relationships, community participation, and reduction in services or calls for service?

If traditional metrics like arrest numbers are the sole metric, responders may not be motivated to pursue a community-oriented approach.

Are de-escalation techniques taught, practiced, and advocated?

The concept of de-escalation is often interpreted as avoiding conflict through nonenforcement of laws. This interpretation misses the mark. De-escalation does not mean avoiding enforcement, nor does it mean people will not be held accountable for their actions. De-escalation means finding ways to accomplish emergency response goals while avoiding unnecessary conflict and situations that have the potential to escalate out of control.

In order to utilize this material to the fullest, one will want to view this book through all four of the lenses: individual, department, community, and policy. To use this book solely to assist with individual interactions may help a first responder in the present, but it will do little for the department and community in the long term. Significant policy changes that affect policing methods based on this training and information will most certainly seem revolutionary to some. Policies must be in place to support and defend such groundbreaking initiatives.

Increasing Self-Awareness and Owning Your Experience

The second objective of this mental model is to become aware of what your personal experience of the societal system has been. First responders who are viewed as good leaders in all the different economic communities are often aware of their experience within the societal system and understand that the people they manage have had different experiences. When you own your personal experience of the system, then you can come to the table and teach others, as well as learn from those who have had different experiences.

A societal system includes these four major components: individuals, institutions, communities, and policies. It may have other elements, but these four major components must be present. Societal systems almost always operate in such a way that one group becomes normalized while others do not. By "normalized" I mean that the norms of one group are assumed to be the norms of society at large. Sometimes this happens unintentionally; sometimes it is very intentional. If you are part of the normalized group, you may be reaping benefits without even being conscious of it. In order to be the most effective leader, you will have to become aware of what your experience of the societal system has been, be willing to own it, and then be willing to come to the table and work with others who have had different experiences.

Let's use an example to further break down this point: When I present this material to an audience, I ask them to raise their hands if they are left-handed. (In the interest of full disclosure, I should note that I learned this activity from the Minnesota Collaborative Anti-Racism Initiative.) Then I ask the left-handed folks, "Has our societal system normalized left-handedness or right-handedness?" The audience always responds, "Right-handedness!"

I continue: "If our societal system normalizes right-handedness, and if you are right-handed like me, then we should expect to find some things that are geared toward us, some benefits we receive simply because we are right-handed. What are some things that are geared toward right-handed people?" Answers such as notebooks, school desks, sporting equipment, kitchen utensils, door handles, credit card machines, and guns are fairly common. All of these are things that are made for people who are right-handed and have to be adjusted (or adjusted to) if the user is left-handed. I have presented this material for years, and every year people mention new things that have been designed for me as a right-handed person that I have never noticed. But the main point is that I didn't have to notice. The societal system has normalized right-handedness. I am right-handed, part of the normalized group, and therefore I receive benefits I am not aware of.

Middle Class: The U.S. Norm?

Apply this example to class. We have normalized middle class in the United States. I have asked families of four making approximately $19,000 a year what class they are in, and they responded, "Middle class." I asked families of four in the same region making more than $150,000 a year what class they are in, and the response was, "Middle class." Middle class is the class that many Americans want to be a part of. It is possible then that there are benefits people in middle class may receive simply because they are in middle class. Look again at the hidden rules of language, and ask yourself which hidden rules and which register of language are most often used in schools, banks, businesses, and emergency response. Middle class rules and formal register are most prevalent; thus, one who grows up in middle class has a built-in advantage when navigating those systems. This is a benefit to that person whether that person realizes it or not.

Many people have, in at least one area of their lives, experienced the benefits of being part of the norm, while in still another area they are not part of the norm. Kirby Moss writes about this very point in his book *The Color of Class: Poor Whites and the Paradox of Privilege.* As a man who is very well educated and makes a higher than average income, he talks about the benefits he has. Still, as a man of color, there are situations in which he does not experience the benefits of being part of the normalized group. For example, when he happens to be the only person of color in a working class bar in a primarily White town, the situation does not allow him to enjoy the benefits of being well educated and having a higher than average income. In this situation he is not part of the norm because his race trumps the benefits he may get from other areas.[28]

It is important to become aware of your experience of the societal system and to move toward ownership of that experience. This is not an afternoon activity; it tends to be a lifetime journey. It is crucial to being an effective leader. Moving toward ownership often requires one to process different emotions. For example, sometimes left-handed people are full of emotion, even angry, when they begin to discuss the various things that are designed for right-handed people and that exclude the left-handed. Likewise, when unaware right-handed people hear these complaints, they too start to get emotional—they start to feel guilty. I have heard right-handed people say, "Oh, I never knew that! I'll make some calls and try to change it!" Both parties must move through their emotions in order to take ownership. Owning your experience can mean acknowledging that you have received benefits that may have been inaccessible to others based on societal norms or acknowledging the difficulty of adjusting to a system in which you are not part of the norm.

Once both parties own their experiences within the societal system, we can set a table in the community where we will listen to those who have had different experiences of that same community. If I own my experience, and a man my age from my community starts to talk about what it is like to be a man in our community, I don't talk over him. When I own my experience, I can say I don't know what it is like to be a man. That man gets to teach me. I don't respond out of my guilt over not knowing or out of my indignation at his perceived benefits; I listen and try to understand. If he owns his experience, then when I talk about what it is like to be a woman in this community, he listens.

When both parties own their experiences, they are more willing to listen to and learn from each other, and that is when a dialogue of mutual respect can take place. Establishing a dialogue of mutual respect will cause first responders to be seen and treated as leaders. This type of leader receives the community's respect and trust. All of this will make the job easier, allow you to be more effective, and keep you safer.

Class: Bringing Everyone to the Table

It is important to note that class is one of the last areas in which the normalized group has no problem telling the other groups what to do and how to do it. In other areas (such as race, gender, and age) it has become politically incorrect for the normalized group to tell the other groups what to do. For example, when the social service, medical, and criminal justice systems started new programs that targeted people from poverty, were there any people from poverty at the table during the creation of those programs? Or was it primarily one group of people from one class using their experience of the societal system to formulate solutions to the problem and then telling another group to conform to the conditions required by the solutions? As we discussed before, it is often ineffective for one person or group of people to tell another group what the problem and solution are without any input from the other groups involved.

The following are examples that further illustrate this point. If a group of men came into a room full of women and told them, "Ladies, our men's group has put together a support group for you women because we understand that it's difficult to be a woman in the United States, and we want to tell you what it's like and support you," right away many women would start to laugh and think, "Yeah, I'm going to come to your support group just to see what you put together."

Very similarly, if a group of White people told a group of Black, Indigenous, and people of color (BIPOC), "Hey, we put together a support group for you because we understand there is still racism in our country, so come to our support group for you," again, many people who identify as BIPOC might laugh and say, "Oh, we're going to come just to see what you put together." Still, we often have only middle class people at the table putting together programs for people in poverty, and we never think twice about it. Class is one of the last areas in which the normalized group, middle class people, still has no problem telling the "other" group, people in poverty, what their problems are and creating solutions for them without seeking any input from them. The solutions created in these conditions are based on the middle class experience of the societal system, which we now understand is very different from that of poverty or wealth. In the cases of other "-ism" areas (like gender, age, and race), this is viewed as politically unacceptable, if not an outright injustice. When addressing any "-ism," all people affected will need to be at the table to contribute to the solutions.

A Story from Gary Rudick

I often tell the following story about how I received an education on bringing the right people to the table when discussing policing tactics.

When I was chief of police for the largest school district police force in Oklahoma, I once received a call from a high school principal who was experiencing a phenomenon within his cafeteria. Huge food fights would break out, and they eventually led to physical assaults and property damage, not to mention the absolute mess. These were not just a few tossed globs of mashed potatoes. This was chair throwing, trash cans turned over, tables tipped, food on the floor, and mass eruptions of physical fights that had the cafeteria staff paralyzed, locking themselves in their kitchen.

The call from the principal was a demand for action. He was convinced the students responsible were gang members who were trying to take over the school. The principal stated he knew who the gang members were, and he wanted law enforcement to force these students out of the school and off campus. He was confident the expulsion of the bad actors would solve the problem. I agreed to attend a meeting with his staff and with the police officer assigned to the school. We met in an empty classroom at the end of the school day.

When we had all arrived and were seated in the classroom, I asked if everyone was present who had a stake in this event. The principal stated everyone was there who should be there, but the police officer assigned to the school quietly said that Maggie was not there. When I asked who Maggie was, I was told she was the cafeteria manager. She had been employed in the school cafeteria for more than 25 years, working her way up from a part-time position to manager of the cafeteria.

I asked the officer to retrieve Maggie for the meeting. The principal, who was new to the building, sighed a heavy sigh of objection, but we waited.

When Maggie arrived and entered the room, I introduced myself, and she quickly proclaimed, "This is about pizza day, ain't it?"

I was surprised and asked, "What do you mean?"

Maggie said, "Every time we have pizza, the football boys push everyone out of the way and get all the pizza. Once all the pizza is gone, kids are mad, and they start fighting, throwing food, and making a mess."

"What should we do?" I asked. "Maggie, are you saying we don't have a gang problem?"

"This ain't no gang problem. Just buy more pizza!" she snorted. Then she looked right at the new principal. "I've told you that."

To solve the problem, we did a few things based on Maggie's recommendation. We bought more pizza on pizza days, we put more employees in the cafeteria, and anyone caught throwing food was sent to detention with a PB&J and an apple to eat all alone. After two weeks, we did not have a single repeat event. Not one. Better yet, there were no suspensions, no arrests, no more fights. I thought Maggie needed a pay raise.

***

It is important to note that though this book is not designed to address all the "-isms" of the communities you serve (sexism, racism, ageism, heterosexism, etc.), it is in your best interest to continue to gain knowledge about these areas because you will deal with them (and their legacies) frequently. The framework we put together to better understand economic class is one that can *begin* our journey to better understanding other "-isms," such as sexism and racism. The field of emergency response is made up of people who are predominantly White and male.[29] It is the authors' sincere hope that as we gain knowledge and understanding about how economic class has impacted ourselves and the communities in which we live and work, ultimately we will apply this framework to better understand intersections with race, gender, and more.

Recall the left-handed, right-handed example. Right-handedness is normalized, and the societal system perpetuates its privilege. People who are right-handed receive benefits because the things they use are designed for right-handed people. Now, think about autonomy. Ask a cisgender male civilian what things he does or thinks about during the day to stay safe. Workshop audiences usually have no more than three responses. Ask a cisgender female, trans, or nonbinary civilian what things they do or think about during the day to stay safe, and there will be a minimum of 15–50 concrete responses. The responses range from "don't walk by myself at night" to "always take a picture of the license plate of the car from a car service company and text it to my friend."

Ask a person who is White what they do to stay safe because of the color of their skin and how that may be perceived on a daily basis or when interacting with first responders. Again, audience member responses range from never having thought about it to about a maximum of five answers (for example, always say "sir" or "ma'am," keep my hands visible on the steering wheel, don't make too big of a deal since I can make my voice heard later by complaining to a supervisor or the courts). Ask someone who identifies as BIPOC what they do to stay safe because of the color of their skin and how that may be perceived on a daily basis or when interacting with first responders. The minimum number of answers is 20–75 (for example, keep my hands out of my pockets in stores or when around anyone in authority, smile so people are not afraid of me, wear "business" clothes all the time—even when running an errand, and the list continues). There are different experiences within our societal system between people who are White and cisgender male and people who are not.

Use this book to begin to think about how your experience may be different than someone of a different race or gender. More importantly, use this chapter to begin to discuss the ways we address racism and sexism as individuals and as members of departments and communities at large. How can we better understand our individual differences, name the systemic biases, and work at the institutional, community, and policy levels to address racism and sexism?

This book contains information that can be used when working directly with people from different economic classes within a department or in a community at large. Use the pieces of this book that pertain to your job, but remember to come back to it as you become a senior first responder, are otherwise promoted, or move to another department. Often the focus of the job begins to change the longer we've been at it. Career advancement in the field of emergency response demands that people expand their view, that they move from the level of the individual to the level of the community, and finally that they move to a systemic point of view. First responders, whether police, paramedics, firefighters, sheriffs, EMTs, or any other branch, almost always start their careers by working directly with citizens. It is as important to begin to use this information with a department or community as it is to use it with individuals. All uses will make the job easier, help you to be perceived as a leader, and ultimately keep you and your fellow first responders safer—and that is what is most important to all the people around you who love you.

It is my hope that the information in this book will help make all of your interactions more successful. When we begin to understand that different communities have different economic realities, we can choose responses that respect those realities and keep us safe. Thank you for all that you do and face every day.

Appendix A
Mental Health Issues in Policing and First Response
Angel A. D. Tucker

I would like to start by addressing the twin elephants in the room, post-traumatic stress disorder (PTSD) and continuous traumatic stress (CTS). This topic is no accident. It is not the latest trend or buzzword. In fact, this topic is very dear to me. I am a 10-year veteran of my local police division. I grew up in an under-resourced community surrounded by gangs, drugs, and violence, and I am currently diagnosed with PTSD and CTS.

One of society's major goals is for the community and its emergency responding agencies to coexist seamlessly and without incident. We can all agree that this is a rather ambitious goal and that we have a wide margin of improvement to close. Better communication amongst first responders and the communities we serve is one of the single most critical stepping stones to improving these relationships. The ability to articulate one's state of mind seems simple; however, it becomes more complex as individuals are exposed to unforeseen events that the brain does not ordinarily process. First responders encounter a multitude of situations that are considered traumatic; the same can be said for those living in under-resourced communities.

First responders are expected to live and work in survival mode. Similarly, individuals who live and work in poverty are often in survival mode. These two groups are thrust into a lifestyle of trauma and survival based on exposure to traumatic and stressful encounters. In this way, the lives of first responders and the lives of community members living in poverty are similar—an interesting dynamic that could potentially bridge the gap between them. There are obstacles, however, that preclude viable solutions from materializing. For example, access to healthcare in under-resourced communities generally presents its own set of complexities. This further sets back the community's ability to receive mental health care. For first responders, although access to healthcare is not typically an issue, displaying signs, symptoms, and/or difficulties adjusting after exposure to trauma is not expected, nor is it encouraged. In fact, the mere mention of the effects of trauma or exposure to others' trauma can detonate an arsenal of stigmas that first responders usually do not want attached to them. First responders who express or show signs of trauma-related effects often face ostracization. Fear of ostracization motivates many first responders to try to hide the effects of exposure to trauma, which creates a lot of unknowns.

How is exposure to trauma addressed and/or communicated? What resources are available, if any? Does the culture create or cultivate an environment of support that will allow communication around the topic of trauma? How do exposure to trauma and operating in survival mode affect the brain and body? What are the long-term effects for those who are continuously exposed to trauma? For those who live in survival mode for extended periods of time, what are the effects on the brain and body? Why is it important to identify symptoms, address diagnoses, and notify colleagues?

Before I begin to address some of these questions, it is important to understand more about the topics we will discuss in this section.

Trauma: "Exposure to actual or threatened death, serious injury, or sexual violence" including direct experience, witnessing trauma occurring to others, learning that trauma occurred to family or close friends, even "experiencing repeated or extreme exposure to aversive details of traumatic event(s) (e.g., first responders collecting human remains; police officers repeatedly exposed to details of child abuse)."[30]

Post-traumatic stress disorder (PTSD): A mental disorder resulting from exposure to trauma and resulting in intrusion symptoms like recurrent distressing memories, distressing dreams, flashbacks that feel like the trauma is recurring, psychological distress at cues that symbolize or resemble an aspect of the trauma, and physiological reactions to those same cues. There are many more possible signs and symptoms of PTSD listed in the *Diagnostic and Statistical Manual of Mental Disorders* (DSM-5). Some that have a negative effect on first responders' work include "persistent and exaggerated negative beliefs about oneself, others, or the world…feelings of detachment or estrangement from others…irritable behavior and angry outbursts (with little or no provocation)…exaggerated startle response…[and] problems with concentration."[31]

Continuous traumatic stress (CTS): Because PTSD assumes that the trauma or traumas are in the past, there has been a need to address traumas that are ongoing. "Continuous traumatic stress offers one possible way of describing the psychological impact of living in conditions in which there is a realistic threat of present and future danger, rather than only experiences of past traumatic events."[32]

PTSD within first responders and people in poverty is a public health epidemic that most Americans are not aware of.[33] Currently affecting people across the United States, this epidemic stifles learning, communication, and relationship-building skills. It reduces drive and pushes sufferers toward violence, drugs, and/or alcohol abuse—activities that inflict further trauma on those around them. Many times, first responders and people in poverty are not receiving proper diagnoses or sufficient treatment. The lack of awareness and funding to address this issue has adversely impacted our systems and communities severely. In fact, the rate of documented PTSD and CTS diagnoses among first responders and underserved youth in this country is even greater than the rate diagnosed in U.S. troops returning home from war.[34] Education on the signs and symptoms of PTSD and CTS is critically important, especially in public safety and school systems, where the signs are typically uncovered first. The families of first responders and people in poverty would also benefit from acquiring knowledge on PTSD and adjustment disorder and how they can work together as a family to cope with the symptoms. Education and support around PTSD and CTS within public safety systems and programs that serve people in poverty are greatly needed and long overdue.

Fighting the War on PTSD

War is defined as a conflict carried on by force of arms, as between nations or between parties within a nation. Domestically, there is conflict carried on by force in urban communities across the United States. As a result, one out of three children that live in violent urban neighborhoods have PTSD and/or suffer continuous traumatic stress.[35] On a national level, PTSD and CTS rates among public safety workers have not been extensively studied. However, smaller studies show that anywhere between 6.5% and 37% of first responders may suffer from PTSD and/or CTS.[36] It is safe to assume that at some point in their career, first responders will most likely be exposed to trauma. The Substance Abuse and Mental Health

Service Administration (SAMHSA) provided an estimate that one out of three first responders develop PTSD.[37] Due to the lack of awareness and attention to the subject, most Americans are unable to understand or address this issue, and that makes it difficult to enact policies that could help.

Howard Spivak, director of the Centers for Disease Control and Prevention's Division of Violence Prevention, stated, "Youth living in inner cities show a higher prevalence of post-traumatic stress disorder than soldiers."[38] Society may occasionally hear about PTSD; however, it is usually in regard to our brave soldiers returning home from war zones in foreign countries. The idea that children in the United States can exhibit higher rates of the disorder than soldiers is hard to fathom.

In 2020 I wrote an article titled "PTSD and CTSD Within First Responders and Inner-City Youth" in which I explain that in both public safety work and under-resourced communities, mental health is low on the list of priorities for survival.[39] Lack of adequate healthcare and health insurance, fear of judgment, perception, stereotypes, and stigmas are just a few of the obstacles to procuring or even prioritizing mental health services. In under-resourced communities and in the public safety community, the law of the land states that only the strong survive. It is considered taboo or a sign of weakness to address any possibility of the mental health effects of trauma. Perception of strength and power is very important in both environments and must be achieved and maintained with little emphasis on the cost to self. This hidden rule in both communities causes community members to feel they must make sacrifices to keep their communities and families safe from harm and that they cannot discuss the negative mental health effects of their sacrifices.

Acquisition of power in under-resourced neighborhoods is often one of the only ways to secure protection and status. This is made very clear during an interview in an article titled "Pathways to Early Violent Death: The Voices of Serious Violent Youth Offenders," in which a 17-year-old male named Mo stated, "I have put in too much work [violence and crime] in my 'hood' to give it up [respect and reputation] to some other dude. Plus, I got a family name to protect...'cause they killed my brother, so I can't be soft in no way."[40] The importance of exercising dominion and building alliances with certain groups in the neighborhood is a hidden rule of power that the youth learn very early in life. When compounded with trauma, it can have grave consequences.

The popular culture shows under-resourced communities (especially under-resourced urban communities comprising mostly Black, Indigenous, and people of color) that fear, violence, and money lead to power. In the pursuit of power, these neighborhoods have become war zones, causing the communities to suffer from an epidemic of PTSD that they are not even aware exists. The fact that the communities are under-resourced and underinformed about the root causes of the crisis reduces their chances of successfully addressing it. The same can be said about the views taken by first responders.

Early in first responders' careers, they are taught that showing fear not only creates vulnerability and risks but also is career suicide. Whether someone is fighting fires, enforcing laws, triaging medical emergencies, or addressing natural disasters, the appearance of control must be upheld. If the community observes any signs of hesitation or fear, they will doubt you. If your fellow responders observe the same, they will also doubt your abilities. Most first responders' number one priority is to make it home safely to their families every night. If a member of the team has a reputation for showing what is perceived to be fear or weakness, this can possibly place that priority in jeopardy. This may affect the responder in several ways. For example, a responder may feel pressure to always appear brave and in control when they are not. The built-up pressure can cause performance anxiety. This can lead to poor and/or dangerous decision-making in the field. Another example is that most responders feel most comfortable at home. The release valve for their stress may be opened at home, causing them to take it out on family members. Or they could attempt to self-medicate with drugs and/or alcohol.

In addition to the pressure of protecting the public and returning home safely, the community looks to first responders as the authority figures, and often saviors, in an emergency. There are times when authority is achieved through dominance, which could be physical or verbal. This places first responders in a precarious position. After repeated successes with this practice, exerting dominance may become the primary tactic used, regardless of necessity. When force is used as the primary tactic, the results are usually conflict. Responders run toward emergency after emergency and conflict after conflict, and they experience trauma after trauma. Because the workplace culture of emergency responders does not allow them to exhibit the effects of fear or trauma, many responders remain uninformed about the negative consequences of repeated exposure to trauma. This reduces the chances of successful interventions. The hidden rule about power for first responders is similar to the hidden rule about power in under-resourced communities: In order to be successful, one must assume and exert power. If the two communities that suffer the most from this epidemic of power exercised through violence will not address it, why should the rest of the country?

Stigmas, Misdiagnoses, and Pitfalls

In the rare cases when a problem is identified and a first responder or member of an underserved community does seek help, they may be misdiagnosed. They are often told they suffer from depression, attention deficit hyperactivity disorder (ADHD), unpredictability, or (in youth cases) are just unruly.[41] If an inaccurate diagnosis is given, the patient will begin a long journey down the road of inadequate treatment while continuing to be exposed to trauma. In a KPIX 5 news piece, Wendy Tokuda discusses the lack of recognition the issue of misdiagnosis is receiving from the medical community. In relation to youth in under-resourced urban neighborhoods, PTSD is sometimes relabeled "hood disease," which compels people outside under-resourced urban neighborhoods to believe it is not a real concern.[42] Calling PTSD "hood disease" also downplays the severity of the crisis within under-resourced communities and delegitimizes any effort to eradicate it. Because there is not enough attention paid to PTSD in under-resourced urban communities, there is not enough funding to address it. People in these communities will continue to be judged and misdiagnosed without regard to their exposure to trauma and violence. When people are labeled deviant, unruly gang members, drug dealers, and criminals, that is how they begin to see themselves, even if they have never engaged in those activities. Analogously, when first responders are labeled abnormal, reckless, unstable, or weak, this is how they begin to see themselves even if they have never displayed such traits.

When first responders or people from poverty exhibit irritability, angry outbursts, aggressive behavior, trouble concentrating, difficulty sleeping, or other edgy behaviors, society reacts with surprise and a lack of empathy. Kataoka et al. state that 75% of youth with PTSD will develop additional mental health disorders that result in this type of conduct.[43] In an article titled "Intervening Processes Between Youths' Exposure to Community Violence and Internalizing Symptoms Over Time: The Roles of Social Support and Coping," Rosario et al. agree. Their article states that increased exposure to community violence—intertwined with decreased guardian and peer support and coupled with increased use of defensive and confrontational behavioral coping—is related to symptoms of anxiety, depression, and PTSD.[44] For youths living in these circumstances, their experience reflects how the world really is: In their minds, there is no escape. I can speak to this on a personal level because I was one of these youths with the philosophy that "it just is what it is until it ain't." I believed every neighborhood had gangs, drugs, and violence, and every time I walked out the door or turned on the television, my daily reality was painted as a destiny filled with few to no choices.

C. Wright Mills defined sociological imagination as "the vivid awareness of the relationship between personal experience and the wider society."[45] When under-resourced youths who have repeatedly been exposed to trauma try to move out of poverty, the results are often unsuccessful. Many believe displaying optimism or positivity is meaningless and irrelevant to their daily reality. Despite their perseverance and hard work, society will continue to label them as misfits, so they engage in what they know will help them survive. Their philosophy is that no one cares about or understands the weight they carry; even more profound, these young people have no idea what it is they are going through themselves. They cannot process why they experience hostile behavior, difficulty focusing, anxiety, and sleep deprivation (alongside many other symptoms of PTSD). They may not realize why they retreat to seclusion, participate in high-risk sexual activity, or self-medicate with drugs and alcohol.

PTSD is also prevalent among emergency responders, but the difference between the two groups—first responders and people in under-resourced communities—arises out of their situational awareness.[46] Earlier I referred to how youth from under-resourced communities learn the hidden rule of how money and violence are a direct path to power very early in life. This is because they have situational awareness. Emergency responders willingly enter stressful situations knowing they will possibly encounter trauma. Nevertheless, when the trauma is too great, the fear of appearing weak prevents most from seeking the proper help. Instead, some attempt to self-medicate and as a result may develop substance abuse problems. The use of alcohol and/or drugs may be a coping tool used to compartmentalize or "erase" memories of trauma.

Trauma affects each person differently, but there is an effect. First responders who are exposed to murder, predatory violence, victimization, physical and/or sexual assault, verbal abuse, mental anguish, substance abuse, neglect, racism, classism, or labeling have a difficult time processing any one of these issues or events. Like people in under-resourced communities, on any given day first responders have and/or are dealing with one or more of these issues. If these issues greatly impact the psychology of adults, imagine the impact they have on a child. The developing mind of a child or teenager cannot be expected to process such trauma without severe consequences. When the traumas are concentrated among a dense population like an under-resourced urban neighborhood, the recipe for an aggressive form of PTSD is manifest. The situation becomes crippling to a child's development.

Addressing the Gap

Richardson, Brown, and Van Brakle, in "Pathways to Early Violent Death: The Voices of Serious Violent Youth Offenders," explore the mindset of Black male inner-city youths within correctional institutions. Young males detained in adult jails for serious violent crimes were interviewed with the goal of understanding their experience of violence. According to the authors, the interviewees' "narratives reveal how the code of the street, informal [hidden] rules that govern interpersonal violence among poor inner-city Black male youths, increases the likelihood of violent victimization."[47] The following excerpt from the article illustrates this:

> Interviewer: On a scale of 1 to 10, 1 meaning your neighborhood is safe and 10 meaning that your neighborhood is dangerous...[h]ow would you rate it?

> Malik (aged 16 years): I would rate it a 20. It's always somebody getting shot in my neighborhood.

Kenny (aged 16 years): I would rate it a 10. Two of my friends were murdered right beside me in a drive-by. Somebody drove by shooting, so we all fell on the ground, but they didn't get up; they died right there in front of me.

G (aged 16 years): I would give it a 10. I seen my man [friend] shot in the head right in front of me; he died in my arms.

Mo (aged 17 years): No doubt it would be a 10 maybe 20. I got shot in my neighborhood, and my brother was killed in front of me. He got killed in a new pair of Jordan's [*sic*]. I still have them. I have the sweat suit he was killed in too. It still has the blood on it.[48]

There is a natural assumption that when soldiers encounter these same types of traumatic events that G and Malik speak of, they will need to seek some type of help or therapy to process these traumas. The resources available to these soldiers are well-documented and easily located. That same community support is elusive or nonexistent for under-resourced youth with similar trauma. Far too often, the correctional system becomes the treatment facility for youth from under-resourced communities. The physical danger first responders face is also well-documented, publicized, and often supported with empathy from the public. However, when the trauma is sleepless nights, fits of rage, self-medicating, emotional breakdowns, and/or suicidal thoughts, the community is not as understanding or tolerant when the danger first responders face is not as visible.

With more than 45 years of experience in clinical psychology, Larry Hamme has done considerable work with first responders, veterans, and gang members. Hamme's graduate studies landed him at the University of Toledo, where he became the first African American to earn a Ph.D. with honors in the Department of

Psychology. During an interview with Hamme, I raised several questions, one of which inquired about the impact of trauma on the brain's chemical composition. When exposed to trauma, the body goes into survival mode. This causes the brain to secrete chemicals that delay nonessential long-term processes in the body, such as eating, digestion, development, and procreation. These secretions can also cause toxicities that alter the nervous system and damage the area of the brain that helps control emotion and memory. This can significantly affect an adult's brain capacity. A brain not yet fully developed can and will sustain damage that produces long-term, if not permanent, effects.

The ability to learn and retain information is greatly decreased after exposure to traumatic events, especially if they become a recurring series of events. As a result, when under-resourced youths arrive at school unable to concentrate and display emotional outbursts, they are often shunned and categorized instead of analyzed and diagnosed. For under-resourced students, learning can regularly take a back seat to their lives outside the classroom. It is extremely difficult to convince a sleep-deprived, traumatized, and/or hungry child that algebra is important. This raises questions concerning a possible link between diminished learning capacity and PTSD.

Hamme suggests better efforts need to be made in training and preparing first responders for the traumas of their work in under-resourced areas where the issues are continuous. Stress inoculation training (SIT) could be used in the field of emergency response. SIT is a form of talk therapy that can help people recognize and change the negative thoughts that influence behavior. Greater efforts to increase public servants' access to solutions like SIT should be implemented through policy and legislation.

Hamme explained that emergency responders' adrenaline levels also create an issue. When exposed to trauma, the body goes into fight-or-flight mode. On a scale of 1–10, the average civilian's situational awareness may keep their adrenaline levels hovering around 1 or 2. If an emergency occurs, those levels will spike. Once the brain and body have determined that there is no longer a threat, the body crashes. During this crash, most people experience fatigue and exhaustion.

However, an emergency responder's situational awareness may keep their adrenaline levels hovering around 4 or 5. First responders understand that the career holds a higher level of danger than others. During a single shift, there may be multiple emergency responses that cause the body's adrenaline levels to spike and drop numerous times. This cycle can carry on for many years, causing the needle to eventually become stuck at the highest level due to prolonged exposure. This poses a risk to personal health and makes receiving proper treatment more complex.

Both first responders and people from poverty face stigma when seeking mental health treatment, but in under-resourced communities, that treatment can also be difficult to obtain. Support groups and programs can help lessen the stigma and provide an entry point to treatment. There are grassroots efforts like this sprouting up around the United States, one being the Urban Warriors project from the YMCA in Chicago, which pairs combat veterans with young people who have been exposed to violence. "These two groups share common life experiences—surviving in hostile environments and striving to cope. Together, they discuss and process their experiences with violence."[49] The goal of the program is to decrease the traumatic effects that violence has on at-risk youth. Urban Warriors delivers a 16-week curriculum involving five areas: belonging, positive character development, intellectual restructuring, coping skills, and community engagement.

The Urban Warriors program inspired the Charles Young Foundation in Toledo, Ohio, to create Project HERO (Helping to Educate, Reconstruct, and Overcome). The Charles Young Foundation promotes and supports education surrounding mental health safety and awareness among first responders and under-resourced youth, specifically in the areas of PTSD and CTS. Project HERO offers a curriculum-based program similar to Urban Warriors, but instead of pairing youths with combat veterans, Project HERO pairs youths diagnosed with PTSD with first responders diagnosed with PTSD. Project HERO provides an environment that supports communication around the topic of trauma. First responders and youths dealing with PTSD come together and share their exposure to trauma, stories about survival, and the difficulty of remaining in violent and hostile environments with little hope of getting out. Together they develop and share coping skills, identify strengths, and examine how to channel those skills and strengths to benefit themselves by discussing and processing their trauma. The program also addresses the importance of physical fitness and community engagement in achieving and maintaining a healthier mental state.

Although the information on PTSD among emergency responders and under-resourced youth is widely available, it is not widely applied, and there is no shortage of critics. Nearly every online resource about PTSD among first responders and youth from poverty is accompanied by comments that suggest a diagnosis of PTSD creates an excuse for lack of performance. Other comments downplay the traumatic experiences encountered, saying they do not compare with combat soldiers' experiences. These responses suggest an underlying issue is lack of awareness. Critics often disproportionately place blame on under-resourced communities. And because first responders' presence is commonplace, people tend to minimize the trauma and danger they face on a regular basis. Attitudes like these are factors in the lack of funding and awareness of this epidemic.

Working Together to Address PTSD and CTS

There is enough research to show that first responders and under-resourced youth are directly affected, and there is enough research to show that PTSD affects brain functionality by stifling learning, communication, and relationship-building skills. Research also demonstrates that drug and alcohol abuse can be directly linked with the effects of PTSD, along with aggression, risky sexual behavior, and a propensity toward violence. Even with all the research into PTSD, there is not enough being done to combat this public health epidemic.

It is important to identify the trauma you, a coworker, or a community member may be coping with. Once it is identified, it can be addressed with the proper treatment. For those who suffer from PTSD, the most difficult element to tackle is letting the people around you know because it can bring on all the presumptions and prejudices associated with mental health. Looking past the stigmas and labels is not easy for people; however, as a first responder, my partner and fellow responders need to be made aware of my diagnosis. Transparency is vital for better understanding potential triggers and/or reactions during traumatic encounters. Informing family members and/or significant others is also essential to the healing process. Lastly, identifying community members who may be reacting to trauma allows responders on scene to use informed decision-making processes.

For the country to move closer to community and first responder collectivity, acknowledgment and appreciation of mental health among first responders and in the wider community must be prioritized. The experiences of first responders and people who have grown up in under-resourced neighborhoods are more similar than different. Unfortunately, many people are quick to assume and blame but slow to insight and solutions. The public sees a "broken" child in an under-resourced neighborhood as an enraged offender who should be incarcerated. It sees police officers as loose cannons, undeserving of their badges. More awareness and acceptance of underlying mental health diagnoses—like PTSD and CTS—could prevent a substantial number of incidents. To begin the healing process, many layers must be addressed, and safe places must be established where people can rebuild their lives without judgment. The prevalence of PTSD and CTS in under-resourced communities and among first responders is not only a crisis but an opportunity to heal together. When we begin to enact legislation, create programming, and allocate funding to diagnose and treat PTSD among youths from poverty and first responders, we will see the dynamics shift. Let this movement begin with you.

Tactical Communication and Community Policing
Gary D. Rudick

If there is one model in emergency response, particularly policing, that is highly pursued by government entities, it is community policing. Community policing is the practice of targeting police response and resources to specific areas of the community and working in partnership with the citizens of the targeted areas, coordinating both public and private resources to solve the underlying problems that contribute to criminal activity. The aim is not only reducing crime but eliminating the causes of repeated offenses, thereby making the community safer. The basis of community policing is a foundation of effective relationships between the police and the citizens of the area. These relationships connect citizens in need with resources in order to improve quality of life. It is no coincidence that relationships are key to persons in poverty and key to a successful community policing program.

Of course, the challenge for responders has always been "the how": how to make those relationships meaningful, how to make them a priority, and how to disengage from practices that hinder relationship building.

For decades now, the most persistent and notorious model of policing has been based on the "broken windows theory." The broken windows model of policing was first described in 1982 in an article by James Q. Wilson and George L. Kelling.[50] They use the analogy of an abandoned commercial building. Someone walks by the building and throws a rock through a window, destroying the glass. Since the building is abandoned, the window is never repaired. The resulting perception is that no one cares that windows are being broken, so other people throw rocks and break out more of the glass. As the overall condition of the building is further neglected, graffiti abounds, and grass and weeds invade the property. When the effects of one broken window were not addressed, more broken windows followed, and eventually the care of the building was abandoned totally. In the same way the untended building is left to ruin, Wilson and Kelling "suggest that 'untended' behavior also leads to the breakdown of community controls."[51] And to think it all started with just a single broken window.

According to the broken window theory, police play a significant role in controlling disorder and reducing feelings of chaos in the community; they are the "tenders" of behavior. Taking care of the little things prevents the little things from becoming bigger things. In short, minor offenses and public order crimes must be aggressively policed as they are the first "broken windows" that lead to more serious crimes. Public order crimes such as public intoxication, vandalism, loitering, littering, and begging are prioritized in order to prevent more serious offenses. Prostitution, illegal gambling, and drug use are public order or morality-based offenses that are also heavily policed, along with zoning offenses such as junk cars, trash, and unmown grass in vacant lots. The theory is that the presence of these violations creates a perception that no one cares about what happens to the neighborhood. If no one cares about the neighborhood, people in the neighborhood think that no one cares what they do as individuals; no one cares if they commit a crime.

But implementing a zero tolerance policy toward public order crimes as a way of preventing more serious crimes may produce a negative return. In short, the broken window theory may be, well, broken. Complaints about zero tolerance policing include:

- It is often in direct conflict with community policing goals. Aggressive enforcement against minor offenses usually does little to create effective relationships with community members.

- Law enforcement is only interested in revenue, and that is what is driving the increase in citations and arrests.

- It disproportionately arrests and incarcerates people in poverty, people with substance abuse problems, and people with mental health issues.

- Incarceration at such a high rate becomes a budgetary burden for state and local governments.

- It promotes socialized mistrust of law enforcement officers, especially among persons in poverty, reinforcing the perception that police are uncaring, unfair, and racially prejudiced. This distrust spreads faster now than ever before through retelling via social media.

Effective policing must take into consideration the impact of such tactics on all economic classes within the community, recognizing that in some cases, application of broken windows policing methods may have a disproportionately negative effect on people in generational poverty. We are seeing a significant portion of our society chafe under these practices. As illustrated in the criticisms listed above, broken windows policing has produced some very bitter fruit.

When attempting to improve the relationships between emergency responders and the community, understanding the impact of decades of the application of the broken windows theory is important for a constructive conversation to occur. This is not to suggest there is no need to enforce laws related to public order crimes, but enforcement must be balanced with the desire to build and maintain quality relationships. This requires other options—not just arrests—for impacting environments that enable the commission of public order crimes.

Meaningful relationships are created when first responders offer solutions to problems that are not simply arrest and incarceration. Can resources be applied to remove trash, hold landowners of vacant properties accountable, enforce zoning laws, connect with faith-based groups to bring people together, and most importantly, listen to what community members themselves see as problems? What are the priorities from the community members' point of view? How would they like to see situations resolved?

In 1992, I was a commanding officer supervising more than 50 personnel per shift for a large municipal police agency. There was one apartment complex in our jurisdiction so plagued with crime that firefighters and medical personnel could not enter without a police escort as they would be attacked by thrown objects, physical assaults, and sometimes gunfire. To counter the problem, we used a "scorched earth" method of policing: Swoop in, arrest everyone we could, leave, and call the problem solved. These aggressive attempts at enforcement produced a lot of arrests but no cooperation from residents. More importantly, complaints against police officers for their conduct and attitude toward the residents were off the charts.

In response, we instituted alternatives to arrest whenever possible and placed two officers on foot patrol in the complex 24 hours a day. These officers were selected for their interpersonal skills and communication abilities. After a year of regular foot patrol, the officers were able to develop meaningful relationships. Social services support, zoning enforcement, and collaboration with the federal Department of Housing and Urban Development and the management of the apartment complex helped to eliminate some of the factors that damaged the overall quality of life. The officers supported a concept of self-governance within the complex that allowed residents to speak out on what they thought needed to happen to make the complex safer.

One evening, a suspected drug dealer in the complex was approached by the two officers, and the suspect ran away. Officers gave chase, and the suspect turned suddenly with a gun in hand. One officer was able to push the suspect backward and gain enough distance to draw his own weapon and fire, killing the suspect. The entire event unfolded right there in the complex, in front of witnesses, and we had every expectation that the community response would escalate into a riot. But that did not happen.

Instead, residents approached the officers and asked about *their* well-being. They showed genuine concern for the officers' safety. Residents were more than willing to share their version of the events, telling everyone around them how the officers had no choice but to defend themselves. The reaction was based on genuine and strong relationships built over time and was significantly different than it likely would have been a year earlier.

In order to be successful, community policing requires the establishment of relationships between emergency responders, citizens, and the people coordinating resources. Having a framework for understanding people in poverty is crucial as well. Applying the theories and information from *Tactical Communication* assists in creating relationships, the key to successful community policing.

Conclusion

Community policing is not only an effective method of combating crime and improving the quality of life for citizens but also a method of policing most desired by the citizens we serve. Successful community policing has three main results:

1. Emergency responders will become more effective in their roles and responsibilities.

2. Citizen and officer safety will improve.

3. Complaints against emergency response employees and their agencies will decrease.

Since we know that relationships are a key to successful community policing and that those same relationships are a driving force for persons in poverty who are the biggest consumers of police services, the ability to create and sustain relationships must be a priority for emergency response agencies. The concepts in *Tactical Communication* help to develop those relationships. Understanding hidden rules, the nuances of language, nonverbal communication, and the importance of resources helps officers develop meaningful relationships.

Endnotes

1 U.S. Census Bureau, "HINC-05"
2 P. E. DeVol, R. K. Payne, and T. Dreussi-Smith, *Bridges Out of Poverty Workbook*
3 C. A. Nadeau, "New Living Wage Data for Now Available on the Tool"
4 P. E. DeVol, R. K. Payne, and T. Dreussi-Smith, *Bridges Out of Poverty Workbook*
5 *Ibid.*
6 R. K. Payne, *A Framework for Understanding Poverty*
7 W. C. Kim and R. Mauborgne, "Fair Process"
8 K. Edin and M. Kefalas, *Promises I Can Keep*
9 K. M. Gilmartin, *Emotional Survival for Law Enforcement,* p. 35
10 M. Mobbs, "An Awful Joke Can Feel Pretty Good"
11 *Ibid.*
12 M. Joos, *The Five Clocks*
13 R. K. Payne, P. E. DeVol, and T. Dreussi-Smith, *Bridges Out of Poverty*
14 *Ibid.*
15 *Ibid.*
16 *Ibid.*
17 R. K. Payne, P. E. DeVol, and T. Dreussi-Smith, *Bridges Out of Poverty;* R. Feuerstein et al., *Instrumental Enrichment*
18 R. K. Payne, P. E. DeVol, and T. Dreussi-Smith, *Bridges Out of Poverty;* E. Berne, *Games People Play*
19 R. K. Payne, *A Framework for Understanding Poverty*
20 P. E. DeVol, *Getting Ahead in a Just-Gettin'-By World*
21 R. K. Payne, P. E. DeVol, and T. Dreussi-Smith, *Bridges Out of Poverty*
22 P. E. DeVol, R. K. Payne, and T. Dreussi-Smith, *Bridges Out of Poverty Workbook*

Endnotes

[23] P. E. DeVol, *Getting Ahead in a Just-Gettin'-By World*

[24] R. Putnam, *Bowling Alone*

[25] R. Jensen, *The Heart of Whiteness*

[26] K. Phillips, *Wealth and Democracy*

[27] J. DeParle, *American Dream*

[28] K. Moss, *The Color of Class*

[29] Zippia, "Emergency Responder Demographics in the U.S."

[30] Substance Abuse and Mental Health Services Administration, "Exhibit 1.3–4, DSM-5 diagnostic criteria for PTSD"

[31] *Ibid.*

[32] American Psychological Association, "Continuous Traumatic Stress"

[33] E. Morris, "Youth Violence"; R. Ebersole, "First Responders Struggle with PTSD Caused by the Emergencies, Deaths, Tragedies They Face Every Day"

[34] N. L. Cole, "Why Inner City Youth Suffer PTSD"

[35] M. Chen, "The PTSD Epidemic in Our Most Violent Neighborhoods"

[36] J. W. Boffa et al., "PTSD Symptoms and Suicidal Thoughts and Behaviors Among Firefighters"

[37] Substance Abuse and Mental Health Services Administration, "First Responders"

[38] KPIX 5, "Inner-City Oakland Youth Suffering from Post-Traumatic Stress Disorder"

[39] A. A. D. Tucker, "PTSD & CTSD Within First Responders and Inner-City Youth"

[40] J. B. Richardson Jr., J. Brown, and M. Van Brakle, "Pathways to Early Violent Death"

[41] B. Zyromski, "African American and Latino Youth and Post-Traumatic Stress Syndrome"

[42] KPIX 5, "Inner-City Oakland Youth Suffering from Post-Traumatic Stress Disorder"

[43] S. Kataoka et al., "Responding to Students with Posttraumatic Stress Disorder in Schools"

[44] M. Rosario et al., "Intervening Processes Between Youths' Exposure to Community Violence and Internalizing Symptoms Over Time"

[45] C. W. Mills, *The Sociological Imagination*

[46] A. A. D. Tucker, "PTSD & CTSD Within First Responders and Inner-City Youth"

[47] J. B. Richardson Jr., J. Brown, and M. Van Brakle, "Pathways to Early Violent Death"

[48] *Ibid.*

[49] YMCA of Metro Chicago, "Youth Safety & Violence Prevention"

[50] G. L. Kelling and J. Q. Wilson, "Broken Windows"

[51] *Ibid.*

Acknowledgments

I would like to thank the St. Paul Police Department in Minnesota for its support of this project—in particular, Chief John M. Harrington (Ret.) and Sergeant Cheryl D. Indehar (Ret.), whose commitment to the development of this content made this book possible. I also thank Chief William K. Finney (Ret.) and Chief Thomas Smith for helping us begin this process. Thanks also are due to Dr. Jan Young and the Assissi Foundation of Memphis, Tennessee. Gratitude to the Memphis Fire Department and the individual firefighters and first responders for their additions. In addition, the following people deserve special thanks for their willingness to meet with me on a regular basis and share their invaluable insight and knowledge: Sheriff Dave Schleve (Ret.), Sheriff Toby Wishard (Ret.), Fire Chief Alvin D. Benson, Lieutenant William S. Fowler (Ret.), Captain Mike Makowski, Lieutenant Larry Ervin, Sergeant Jack Serier, Sergeant Joe Strong, Sergeant Rutha DeJesus, Officer Timothy Bradley, Officer Darryl Hunter, Officer Errol Johnson, Officer Lucia Wroblewski, and Officer Xiong Yang. I also want to thank all of the first responders who were willing to share their stories.

To Dr. Ruby K. Payne, Philip E. DeVol, and Terie Dreussi-Smith, coauthors of *Bridges Out of Poverty,* I thank you for your contributions to the area of understanding the different economic classes and building sustainable communities. A large amount of gratitude goes to the aha! Process publications team for their hard work and patience.

Officer Angel Tucker and Chief Gary Rudick (Ret.) are two men who have given and are giving their all to serve their communities. You two live and work in different regions of the country and have different backgrounds, but both of you, like so many first responders, are giving more of yourselves than the community often is aware of. I thank you for your service and for sharing your wisdom within the book.

Finally, I want to give a deep, heartfelt thank you to everyone who works in emergency service for the challenging job you do every day. It is my hope that this book will help reduce the challenges you face in the job and increase the rewards.

–Jodi Pfarr

References and Suggested Readings

Abram, K. M., Teplin, L. A., Charles, D. R., Longworth, S. L., McClelland, G. M., & Dulcan, M. K. (2004). Posttraumatic stress disorder and trauma in youth in juvenile detention. *Archives of General Psychiatry, 61*(4), 403–410. https://doi.org/10.1001/archpsyc.61.4.403

American Psychological Association. (2013, May). *Continuous traumatic stress.* APA. https://www.apa.org/pubs/journals/special/6041905

Berne, E. (1996). *Games people play: The basic handbook of transactional analysis.* Ballantine Books.

Boffa, J. W., Stanley, I. H., Hom, M. A., Norr, A. M., Joiner, T. E., & Schmidt, N. B. (2017). PTSD symptoms and suicidal thoughts and behaviors among firefighters. *Journal of Psychiatric Research, 84,* 277–283. https://doi.org/10.1016/j.jpsychires.2016.10.014

Boxer, P., Power, E., Mercado, I., & Schappell, A. (2012). Coping with stress, coping with violence: Links to mental health outcomes among at-risk youth. *Journal of Psychopathology and Behavioral Assessment, 34,* 405–414. https://doi.org/10.1007%2Fs10862-012-9285-6

Brito, C. S., & Gratto, E. E. (Eds). (2000). *Problem-oriented policing: Crime-specific problems, critical issues, and making POP work* (Vol. 3). Police Executive Research Forum.

Carrion, V. G., & Wong, S. S. (2012). Can traumatic stress alter the brain? Understanding the implications of early trauma on brain development and learning. *Journal of Adolescent Health, 51*(2 Suppl.), S23–28. https://doi.org/10.1016/j.jadohealth.2012.04.010

Causey, J. E. (2014, June 7). PTSD spikes in inner city youth. *Milwaukee Journal Sentinel.* http://www.jsonline.com/news/opinion/ptsd-spikes-in-inner-city-youth-b99283714z1-262210721.html

Chen, M. (2014, March 4). *The PTSD epidemic in our most violent neighborhoods.* Al Jazeera. http://america.aljazeera.com/opinions/2014/3/ptsd-mental-healthgunviolencetrauma.html

Cole, N. L. (2019, February 3). *Why inner city youth suffer PTSD.* ThoughtCo. https://www.thoughtco.com/hood-disease-is-a-racist-myth-3026666

Covey, S. R. (1989). *The 7 habits of highly effective people: Powerful lessons in personal change.* Simon & Schuster.

DeParle, J. (2005). *American dream: Three women, ten kids, and a nation's drive to end welfare.* Penguin.

DeVol, P. E. (2006). *Facilitator notes for* Getting ahead in a just-gettin'-by world: Building your resources for a better life (2nd ed.). aha! Process.

DeVol, P. E. (2006). *Getting ahead in a just-gettin'-by world: Building your resources for a better life* (2nd ed.). aha! Process.

DeVol, P. E., Payne, R. K., & Dreussi-Smith, T. (2006). *Bridges out of poverty: Strategies for professionals and communities workbook.* aha! Process.

Ebersole, R. (2019, October 26). First responders struggle with PTSD caused by the emergencies, deaths, tragedies they face every day. *Washington Post.* https://www.washingtonpost.com/health/first-responders-struggle-with-ptsd-caused-by-the-emergencies-deaths-tragedies-they-face-every-day/2019/10/25/9c4c9a0e-d4b8-11e9-9610-fb56c5522e1c_story.html

Edin, K., & Kefalas, M. (2011). *Promises I can keep: Why poor women put motherhood before marriage.* University of California Press.

Erbentraut, J. (2015, May 29). *School may be the best place to address PTSD in young people, but resources are spread thin.* Huffington Post. http://www.huffingtonpost.com/2015/05/29/urban-youth-ptsd-schools_n_7337158.html

Feuerstein, R. (with Rand, Y., Hoffman, M. B., & Miller, R.). (1980). *Instrumental enrichment: An intervention program for cognitive modifiability.* University Park Press.

Gilmartin, K. M. (2002). *Emotional survival for law enforcement: A guide for officers and their families.* E-S Press.

Jensen, R. (2005). *The heart of Whiteness: Confronting race, racism, and White privilege.* City Lights.

Joos, M. (1967). *The five clocks: A linguistic excursion into the five styles of English usage.* Harcourt, Brace, & World.

Joos, M. (1972). The styles of the five clocks. In R. D. Abrahams, & R. C. Troike (Eds.), *Language and cultural diversity in American education* (pp. 145–149). Prentice-Hall.

Kataoka, S., Langley, A., Wong, M., Baweja, S., & Stein, B. (2012). Responding to students with posttraumatic stress disorder in schools. *Child and Adolescent Psychiatric Clinics of North America, 21*(1), 119–133. https://doi.org/10.1016/j.chc.2011.08.009

Kelling, G. L., & Wilson, J. Q. (1982, March). Broken windows: The police and neighborhood safety. *The Atlantic.* https://www.theatlantic.com/magazine/archive/1982/03/broken-windows/304465/

Kim, W. C., & Mauborgne, R. (2003, January). Fair process: Managing in the knowledge economy. *Harvard Business Review.* https://hbr.org/2003/01/fair-process-managing-in-the-knowledge-economy

KPIX 5. (2014, May 16). *Inner-city Oakland youth suffering from post-traumatic stress disorder.* CBS Local. http://sanfrancisco.cbslocal.com/2014/05/16/hood-disease-inner-city-oakland-youth-suffering-from-post-traumatic-stress-disorder-ptsd-crime-violence-shooting-homicide-murder/

Lui, M., Robles, B., Leondar-Wright, B., Brewer, R., & Adamson, R. (2006). *The color of wealth: The story behind the U.S. racial wealth divide.* New Press.

McCall, N. (1995). *Makes me wanna holler: A young Black man in America.* Random House.

Miller, W. R., & Rollnick, S. (2002). *Motivational interviewing: Preparing people for change* (2nd ed.). The Guilford Press.

Mills, C. W. (1959). *The sociological imagination.* Oxford University Press.

Mobbs, M. (2018, May 10). *An awful joke can feel pretty good.* Psychology Today. https://www.psychologytoday.com/us/blog/the-debrief/201805/awful-joke-can-feel-pretty-good

Morris, E. (2009). *Youth violence: Implications for posttraumatic stress disorder in urban youth.* National Urban League Policy Institute. Policy Archive. http://research.policyarchive.org/17613.pdf

Moss, K. (2003). *The color of class: Poor Whites and the paradox of privilege.* University of Pennsylvania Press.

Nadeau, C. A. (2020, March 3). *New living wage data for now available on the tool.* Massachusetts Institute of Technology Living Wage Calculator. https://livingwage.mit.edu/articles/61-new-living-wage-data-for-now-available-on-the-tool

Nebbitt, V. E., Lombe, M., Yu, M., Vaughn, M. G., & Stokes, C. (2011). Ecological correlates of substance use in African American adolescents living in public housing communities: Assessing the moderating effects of social cohesion. *Children and Youth Services Review, 34*(2), 338–347. https://doi.org/10.1016/j.childyouth.2011.11.003

Pascale, R. T., & Sternin, J. (2005, May). Your company's secret change agents. *Harvard Business Review.* https://hbr.org/2005/05/your-companys-secret-change-agents

Payne, R. K. (2005). *A framework for understanding poverty* (4th ed.). aha! Process.

Payne, R. K. (2005). *A framework for understanding poverty workbook* (2nd ed.). aha! Process.

Payne, R. K. (2019). *A framework for understanding poverty* (6th ed.). aha! Process.

Payne, R. K., DeVol, P. E., & Dreussi-Smith, T. (2006). *Bridges out of poverty: Strategies for professionals and communities* (3rd ed.). aha! Process.

Phillips, K. (2003). *Wealth and democracy: A political history of the American rich.* Broadway Books.

Putnam, R. (2001). *Bowling alone: The collapse and revival of American community.* Simon & Schuster.

Richardson, J. B. Jr., Brown, J., & Van Brakle, M. (2013). Pathways to early violent death: The voices of serious violent youth offenders. *American Journal of Public Health, 103*(7), e5–e16. https://doi.org/10.2105/AJPH.2012.301160

Rosario, M., Salzinger, S., Feldman, R.S., & Ng-Mak, D.S. (2007). Intervening processes between youths' exposure to community violence and internalizing symptoms over time: The roles of social support and coping. *American Journal of Community Psychology, 41*(1–2), 43–62. https://doi.org/10.1007/s10464-007-9147-7

Substance Abuse and Mental Health Services Administration. (2014). Exhibit 1.3–4, DSM-5 diagnostic criteria for PTSD. *Trauma-Informed Care in Behavioral Health Services.* Treatment Improvement Protocol (TIP) Series, No. 57. National Center for Biotechnology Information. https://www.ncbi.nlm.nih.gov/books/NBK207191/box/part1_ch3.box16/

Substance Abuse and Mental Health Services Administration. (2018, May). First responders: Behavioral health concerns, emergency response, and trauma. *Disaster*

Technical Assistance Center Supplemental Research Bulletin. https://www.samhsa.gov/sites/default/files/dtac/ supplementalresearchbulletin-firstresponders-may2018.pdf

Tucker, A. A. D. (2020). *PTSD & CTSD within first responders and inner-city youth.* Charles Young Foundation. https:// charlesyoungfoundation.org/ptsd%2F-tactical-comm-1/f/ptsd-ctsd-with-in-first-responders-and-inner-city-youth

U.S. Census Bureau. (2020). HINC-05: Percent distribution of households, by selected characteristics within income quintile and top 5 percent. Current Population Survey, 2020 Annual Social and Economic Supplement. https://www.census.gov/ data/tables/time-series/demo/income-poverty/cps-hinc/hinc-05.html

YMCA of Metro Chicago. (2021). *Youth safety & violence prevention: Urban warriors.* YMCA Chicago. https://www. ymcachicago.org/programs/youth-safety-and-violence-prevention-urban-warriors

Zippia. (2021, January 29). *Emergency responder demographics in the U.S.* Zippia. https://www.zippia.com/emergency-responder-jobs/demographics/

Zyromski, B. (2007). African American and Latino youth and post-traumatic stress syndrome: Effects on school violence and interventions for school counselors. *Journal of School Violence, 6*(1) 121–137. https://doi.org/10.1300/ J202v06n01_08

About the Authors

Jodi R. Pfarr, M.Div. is an author, speaker, trainer, and CEO of J Pfarr Consulting. She formerly served as a certified critical debriefer and chaplain for the St. Paul Police Department in Minnesota and is well familiar with police culture and the daily challenges faced by police officers. Pfarr carried out vast trainings with the St. Paul Police Department and the Memphis Fire Department (Tennessee) and held many subsequent interviews with personnel within and those and other departments. Those trainings and interviews contributed to many of the illustrations contained in this book. Pfarr is the coauthor of *The Urgency of Awareness: Unlocking the Power Within Individual, Organizational, and Community Efforts.*

Gary D. Rudick is a 35-year veteran of law enforcement in Oklahoma, serving the citizens of the state as a patrol officer, supervisor, and chief of police. He has a master's in criminal justice and is a graduate of the FBI National Academy, Session 242. As chief of police, he led one police agency to receive the 2006 International Association of Chiefs of Police Civil Rights Award and achieve state accreditation, implementing best practices in policing.

In 2008, Rudick was tasked with creating the largest public school policing agency in Oklahoma, serving more than 40,000 students and 6,000 employees. His approach and organizational structure for a public school policing entity has been emulated across the nation.

In 2013, Rudick served on the Oklahoma lieutenant governor's Oklahoma Commission on School Security, which developed key legislation to increase safety and security at schools following the tragedy at Sandy Hook Elementary School in Newtown, Connecticut. He has served as president for the Oklahoma Association of Chiefs of Police (OACP) and was on the board of directors for OACP from 2005 until he retired from law enforcement in 2014. He then accepted a position to serve with the Oklahoma Office of Homeland Security. His work there included a focus on safety for all students, faculty, and staff, as well as instructing law enforcement in areas of education policing, safety, and security until 2019.

Recognized as a leader in school safety and security, Rudick is a certified instructor for the State of Oklahoma Council for Law Enforcement Education and Training and is a published author on school policing in the FBI Law Enforcement Bulletin. He continues to advocate for innovative policing methods based on the recommendations found in *Tactical Communication.*

Angel A. D. Tucker was born and raised in Toledo, Ohio. He grew up in an impoverished neighborhood flooded with drugs, gangs, and violence. Rather than falling victim to these pressures, Tucker persevered, becoming a notable servant of his community for more than 30 years. Tucker helped organize neighborhood revitalization initiatives. He has since been dedicated to mentoring youths from similar communities.

In 2011, Tucker made local history by becoming the first African American police officer to join the Oregon Police Department (OPD) in Oregon, Ohio, where he currently serves as patrolman. Tucker is currently working on an initiative with the OPD, city officials, and Bowling Green State University to recruit a more diverse slate of candidates for first responders across the county. Tucker has served on the SWAT Team, Crisis Intervention Team (CIT), Crisis Negotiator Unit (CNU), Drug Abuse Response Team (DART) Honor Guard, and Bike Patrol Unit and is currently a presenter for the Citizens Police Academy.

Tucker is highly regarded as a leader and advocate in the field of mental health. His mission to bring awareness to post-traumatic stress disorder (PTSD) and continued traumatic stress (CTS) has been acknowledged and integrated into his Tactical Communication work. These efforts have been recognized locally by the mental health board and other organizations, earning him the 2020 Officer of the Year award for Lucas County, Ohio. To further support people who suffer with PTSD, Tucker and his wife founded the Charles Young Foundation. Learn more at charlesyoungfoundation.org.

Connect with us at ahaprocess.com

- **Visit ahaprocess.com for free resources: articles, video clips, and success stories from practitioners—and read our aha! Moments blog!**

- **Sign up for our latest LIVE online workshop offerings at ahaprocess.com/events:**
  - Tactical Communication Workshop for First Responders
  - Bridges Out of Poverty Workshop and Trainer Certification
  - Emotional Poverty Workshops and Trainer Certification
  - Bridges Across Every Divide Workshop
  - Getting Ahead in a Just-Gettin'-By World Facilitator Training
  - Register for on-demand workshops at ahaprocess.com/on-demand

- **If you like *Tactical Communication,* check out these publications:**
  - *Bridges Out of Poverty: Strategies for Professionals and Communities* (Payne, DeVol, & Dreussi-Smith)
  - *A Framework for Understanding Poverty: A Cognitive Approach* (Payne)
  - *Emotional Poverty in All Demographics* (Payne)
  - *How Much of Yourself Do You Own? A Process for Building Your Emotional Resources* (Payne & O'Neill-Baker)
  - *Bridges Across Every Divide: Policy and Practices to Reduce Poverty and Build Communities* (DeVol & Krebs)
  - *Workplace Stability: Creating Conditions That Lead to Retention, Productivity, and Engagement in Entry-Level Workers* (Weirich)

- **Connect with us on Facebook, Twitter, and Instagram— and watch our YouTube channel**

For a complete listing of products, please visit ahaprocess.com

Join us on Facebook
facebook.com/rubypayne
facebook.com/bridgesoutofpoverty

 Twitter
@rubykpayne
@ahaprocess
#addresspoverty
#BridgesOutofPoverty

 Subscribe to our YouTube channel
youtube.com/ahaprocess

 Read our blog
ahaprocess.com/blog

 Instagram
@ rubykpayne